South India

the land of

SALIM PUSHPANATH

SARASWATHY RAJAGOPALAN

Presented by

 Indian Panorama 

www.indianpanorama.in

South India

Photography & Concept: Salim Pushpanath

Text: Saraswathy Rajagopalan

Pre-press Colortone Process Pvt Ltd

Pre-press & Color Management: Brijilal

Acknowledgment:This book would not have been possible without Mr.K M Azeez

For overseas rights and sales, please contact the publisher.

Printed and bound by Times Offset (M) Sdn Bhd, Malaysia

Published by Salim Pushpanath
DEE BEE INFO PUBLICATIONS
"Pushpanath" Malloossery, Kottayam - 686 041.

Untouched by the materialistic world around him

A lotus (the national flower of India) in full bloom

South India

The Indian South is a land of myths, mysteries and magnificent structures. The East India Company established a trading post at Chennai (Madras) the capital of Tamil Nadu in the 17th century. Perhaps it was a logical place for the British to start their southern adventure. English is still widely spoken in many parts of the south. The state of Tamil Nadu in southern India has an ancient history dating back over 6000 years before Christ. And it certainly represents the nucleus of the Dravidian culture in India.

For the visitor almost all the roads out of Chennai lead south, except for the road west to Kanchipuram, famous for its heavy silk and temples. The route south, around the tip of India, abounds with a wealth of attractions. The 7th century stone temples at Mahabalipuram (also called Mamallapuram) are one of South India's biggest tourist attractions. Here stands the largest relief sculpture in the world, 'Arjuna's Penance'. The penance relates to the mythical origins of the holy river Ganges in the Himalayas.

The Union Territory of Pondicherry (also known as Puducherry), the last out-post of colonial France in India, is only a two to three hour drive from Mahabalipuram. Further south, are the two great temple cities of Thanjavur (Tanjore), and Madurai. Northwest of Madurai, about 120 km away is Kodaikanal, one of the popular hill resorts of the Western Ghats. Kodaikanal is rivaled only by Ooty (Ootacamund) in the Niligris, a part of the Western Ghats and Nilgiri Biosphere reserve. Both places offer breathtaking views and endless possibilities for outdoor activities. During the Raj the British migrated to the hills in the summer to escape the heat of the coastal plains.

Chettinad: massive, beautifully built homes, elaborate with carvings and paintings, lie uninhabited, their vast spaces echoing with bats' wings and columns of sunlight lying scattered through fine cobwebs.

South of Madurai, India comes to an end in the raging surf of Kanyakumari, at the tip of Cape Comorin, where the Bay of Bengal meets the Indian Ocean and the Arabian Sea.

An hour's drive up the west coast of India from Kanyakumari begins the fascinating Kerala experience. It truly looks like another country and offers an unusual experience, a tropical paradise, amidst a 100% literate, cosmopolitan, yet friendly populace, who were beneficiaries of an odd trinity: progressive rulers, a strong Christian school system and later Communist-led governments. To understand this odd confluence, stop at Padmanabhapuram, near Nagarcoil, on the road to Trivandrum (Thiruvananthapuram) . Padmanabhapuram was once the capital of Travancore, what is now Kerala. This small town is home to one of the finest but often least visited heritage masterpieces in India, The Padmanaphapuram Palace.

The Arabian Sea offers many a lovely beach all along coastal Kerala. A half days drive north of Trivandrum (Thiruvananthapuram), through the backwater town of Kollam (Quilon), and along the coastal town of Alappuzha (Alleppey) often referred to as the 'Venice of the East' is Kochi (Cochin), a beautiful natural harbour. Kumarakom, with its 14-acre bird sanctuary slumbers on the banks of the Vembanad Lake. A visitor could spot water ducks, cuckoos, Siberian storks and many other migratory birds.

Wayanad is emerging as an interesting tourist destination with exclusive tree houses. Some tree house can be reached only by riding on an elephant. Here tourism and nature work in harmony without violating the rule and role of nature. Tourists can angle in the lake nearby and consume organically grown vegetables.

Thekkady is in the district of Idukki, a district of hills, tea, coffee and cardamom plantations and a hydel dam producing electricity for Kerala. Thekkady Tiger Reserve is one of the oldest and most well known sanctuaries in Kerala. It is also an adventure destination, offering a mixed menu of sites and sounds, relaxation and exhilaration, and tremendous opportunities for photography.

Fishing is an integral part of the life and economy of South India

The grand entrance to a Chettinad house

A vaishnavite (devoted to Lord Vishnu) priest in Vishnu Kanchi

An example of the exquisite and detailed sculptures that adorn the temple walls at Somanathapur

The hill stations in the Western Ghats bordering the east coast are relatively cool and almost cold (especially at night) in winter. Most of the original forests (except for a few reserve forests) of rosewood, ebony and teak have been replaced with rice, rubber, tea, coffee, spice plantations and huge dams. Kerala is also famous for its own classical dance forms such as Kathakali, Mohiniyattom and Theyyam apart from of course Ayurveda. Ayurveda, is the ancient Indian health science, a way of life to effectively achieve both mental and physical bliss naturally!

Offshore are the coral islands of Lakshadweep, the tiniest Union Territory of India. Lakshadweep is an archipelago consisting of 12 atolls, three reefs, and five submerged banks. Only 10 of its islands are inhabited. Of these only five are open to visitors of which Bangaram is the most popular and is the only one open to foreigners. Although not a budget traveller's destination, this little visited spot in the Indian Ocean has a unique marine environment with the dive sites undisturbed and the coral intact.

Bordering northern Kerala is the state of Karnataka, the land of primordial forests, ornate shrines and beautifully laid out cosmopolitan cities. It is indeed a state of strong contrasts with a modern industrialized capital city of Bangalore often referred to as the 'Silicon Valley' of India at one extreme and the expanses of rural farming on the other. The city of Mysore is famous for the Dussehra festival, stunning Palaces and the Brindavan Gardens. Among the natural parks is the Bandipur Wild Life Sanctuary 80 km south of Mysore.

The ruins of the once vibrant capital of the Hindu empire of Vijayanagar at Hampi are awe-inspiring. Sravanabelagola where the gigantic 18 m statue of Gomateswara stands is a Jain pilgrim centre. Mangalore is the major port with many an enchanting beach on the Arabian coast.

Bordering north Karnataka is Goa the smallest state in the Indian union. Goa was a Portuguese territory for almost a century, till December 19th 1961. Tourism is a major industry here. Dabolim airport, near the port town of Vasco da Gama, is equipped to receive chartered flights. Calangute, Colava and Vagator are some of the popular beaches. Old Goa has a Basilica of Bom Jesus, where the casket containing the incorruptible body of St. Francis, the Apostle of Goa is entombed.

Tucked away between the Western Ghats and the Arabian Sea, Goa is indeed a paradise with long sunny beaches, miles of mangroves, cashew and coconut palms. The climate is warm and languid with little variation in temperature. Blue and tranquil, this is one beach destination in India where the adventurous can enjoy aquatic sports like parasailing, speed boating, water skiing, yachting, wind surfing and deep sea diving. Those seeking peace and solitude can relax gazing at the endless stretch of blue and unwind. A holiday on the beaches of Goa is an unforgettable experience often unfolding many an unexpected picturesque sight of stunning sunsets and endless moonlit nights.

History

In a recent excavation in the Vindhya Range a worn limestone statue of a goddess sculptured between 25,000 and 15,000 years ago was unearthed. Archaeologists continue to excavate at Hungsi in Karnataka, but nothing has been unearthed so far that surpasses the antiquity of the oldest finds on the Indian subcontinent. According to the archaeologists, hunting and gathering appears to have coexisted with fishing, herding and even small-scale agriculture.

Aryan Invasion

It seems that North and South India evolved quite independently of one another. Excavations in the south, especially in Maharashtra, Tamil Nadu and Karnataka indicate the existence of agricultural patterns that made these regions quite distinct from one another. Great changes occurred in the past during the Aryan invasion. Aryans controlled the whole of northern Indian as far as the Vindhya range and pushed the original inhabitants, the Dravidians, south. The northerners brought their literature, their gods, their language (Sanskrit) and a social structure that divided people into several castes.

Buddhism

The Emperor Ashoka was a major force behind Buddhism's inroads into the south. He sent Buddhist missionaries far and wide. His edicts have been found in Andhra Pradesh and Karnataka. Stupas were also built in southern India, mostly in Andhra Pradesh. One stupa was

A puja thattu, ready to be offered to the Gods

The 58-feet-high statue of Lord Gomateswara at Sravanab

constructed as far south as Kanchipuram in Tamil Nadu under Ashoka's patronage.

Chandragupta's son Bindusara ascended the throne around 300 BC and extended the empire as far as Karnataka. Sangam literary records describe a land known as the 'abode of the Tamils' within which resided three major ruling families, the Pandyas (Madurai) the Cheras (Malabar Coast); and the Cholas (Thanjavur and the Cauvery Valley).

Lalitha Mahal Palace at Mysore

Roman Trade

Trade between western Asia and the west coast of India took place at least 1000 years before Christ. Hebrew texts refer to the port of Ophir located along this same patch of coast line. Babylonian builders as far back as the 7th century BC used Indian teak and cedar. An anonymous Greek document, written sometime in the 1st century, describes various ports along the coast of India. It also give details about the active Roman trade in South India. British archaeologist Sir Mortimer Wheeler during an excavation at Arikkamedu near Pondicherry uncovered a Roman settlement as well as pieces of pottery that had been manufactured near Rome. Pottery made in Tunisia, when it was under Roman control has been uncovered at Rameswaram. In central Kerala in 1983, more than 200 gold coins minted in Rome in the 2nd century were discovered by workers digging for clay to make bricks.

n Karnataka

Cholas and Pallavas

The Kalabhras suppressed Tamil chieftains at first. Soon South India split into numerous warring kingdoms. The Cholas virtually disappeared. The Cheras prospered through trading. The Kalabhras were overthrown late in the 6th century AD. For the next 300 years the history of South India is resplendent with the fortune of the Chalukyas of Badami, the Pallavas of Kanchi and the Pandyas of Madurai. From their base at Thanjavur, the Cholas spread north and absorbed what was left of the territory of the Pallavas and made inroads into the south. Music, dance and literature also flourished, and as a result Tamil culture, acquired a more distinct character, enduring in South India long after the Cholas had disappeared from the picture. Trade wasn't the only thing the Cholas brought to the shores of South East Asia; they also introduced their culture. That legacy lives on in Myanmar (Burma), Bali and Cambodia in the dance forms, religion and mythology of the regions.

Chital - Nagarhole

Muslim rulers

By 1323 AD Muslim rulers had reached Madurai in Tamil Nadu, pushing aside a series of local rulers, including the Hoysalas and Pandyas. Muhammad Tughluq rebuilt the fortifications in Daulatabad in Maharashtra to keep control of southern India, but in 1334 he recalled his army in order to wage campaigns elsewhere. The Vijayanagar Empire is generally said to have been founded by two chieftain brothers who, having been captured and taken to Delhi, where they converted to Islam, were sent back south to serve as governors for the Sultanate. Around 1336 AD the brothers reconverted to Hinduism established a kingdom that was to eventually cover all the areas of southern Karnataka, Tamil Nadu and part of Kerala. Portuguese chronicler Domingo Paez had arrived in Vijayanagar during the reign of one of its greatest kings, Krishnadevaraya. Vasco da Gama arrived in Calicut in 1498 and soon doors were opened for trade between the Portuguese and Indians. After Vasco da Gama Afonse de Albuquerque reached the shores of India and he established his empire that included Goa. The Portuguese also introduced their religion, Roman Catholicism. After the defeat of the Spanish Armada in 1588 AD, the sea route to the east lay open to the English and the Dutch.

Dressed in lights, Mysore Palace during Dussehra

Dutch and Mughals

The Dutch were more interested in trade than they were in religion and empire. They followed a special system to establish trade relations with various countries. The Indonesians wanted textiles for spices, the Indians and Chinese wanted silver for textiles. They set up factories at Surat (Gujarat) and on the Coromandel

A Bharatanatyam dancer strikes a difficult pose

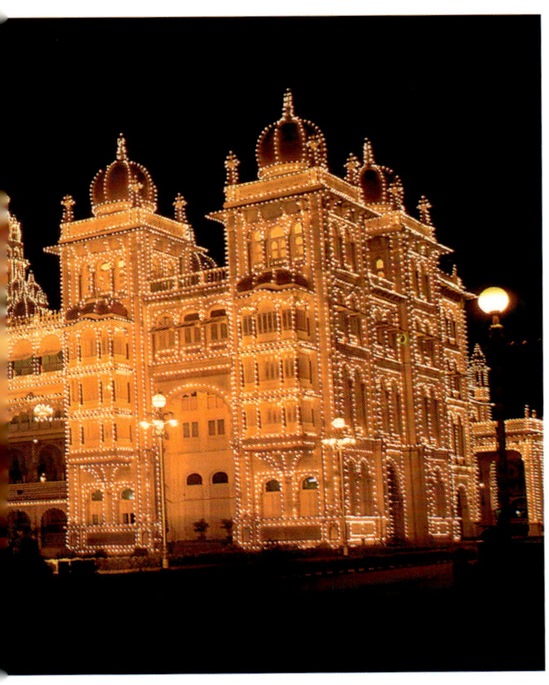

Coast in South India, and entered into a treaty with the ruler of Calicut. In 1660 AD they captured Portuguese forts at Cochin and Cranganore (now known as Kannur).

Delhi-based Mughals made inroads into southern India and captured Bijapur and Golconda. Emperor Aurangzeb captured Thanjavur and set up a capital at Gingee near Madras. After the death of Aurangzeb the Mughal empire showed signs of disintegration. The Marathas acquired more strength and they tried to establish their supremacy in the south. But they discovered that the French were providing military support to the Hyderabadi rulers.

Tipu's Kingdom

In the south, Travancore (Kerala) and Mysore were trying to gain control of important maritime regions. Marthanda Varma of Travancore, in southern Kerala, created his own army and tried to limit the activities of European traders in the region. Under the rule of Rama Varma (Marthanda's son) trade in many goods, with the exception of pepper, became a royal monopoly. A migrant cavalry officer Hyder Ali assumed power in 1761 AD and set about acquiring coastal territory. Hyder Ali and his son Tipu Sultan eventually ruled over a kingdom that included Kodagu (Coorg), coastal Karnataka and northern Kerala. Tipu was killed when the British stormed Seringapatam in 1799 AD. The foundations for the formation of the Madras Presidency was laid by Wellesley when he restored the old ruling family, the Wodeyars, to half of Tipu's Kingdom.

The rest of Tipu's kingdom went to the Nizam of Hyderabad. The British also absorbed Thanjavur and Karnataka. Thus most of India came under British influence. The Madras Presidency stretched all the way from present day Andhra Pradesh in the north to the tip of the subcontinent in the south and from the east coast right across to the Malabar coast in the west. After independence in 1947 the British Residencies and the Madras Presidency were dismantled and South India was reorganised into states along linguistic lines. The boundaries of Mysore state were redrawn in 1956 (under 1956 States Reorganisation Act) and the extended Kannada–speaking state of Greater Mysore was established. This was renamed Karnataka in 1972. In 1987 Goa was officially recognised as the 25th state of the Indian Union. Kerala as it is today, was created in 1956 from Travancore, Cochin and Malabar (formerly part of the Madras Presidency) with many parts of the Telugu-speaking areas of the old Hyderbadi Nizam's territory. Tamil Nadu emerged from the

The temple walls at Somanathapur

Theyyam-This is a ritual dance form

The exquisite murals-at Ettumanur Temple

old Madras Presidency. It lost Malabar district and South Canara to the state of Kerala in the reorganisation of states in 1956. However it also gained new areas in Trivandrum district, including Kanyakumari. In 1960 some land in Andhra Pradesh was exchanged for a similar portion of land in Salem and Chengalpattu districts. The French handed over Pondicherry in 1947 and it remains a Union Territory of India.

Symbolic Division

The Vindhya Range, which stretches across nearly the entire width of peninsular India, symbolically divides the north and south. South of the Vindhya Range lies the Deccan Plateau, a triangular–shaped mass of ancient rock that slopes gently eastward towards the Bay of Bengal. Southern rivers such as the Godavari, Krishna and the Cauvery originate in the rain-soaked peaks of the Western Ghats. The Western Ghats start to rise just north of Mumbai and run parallel to the coast, until they reach the tip of the peninsula. Here they merge with the southern-most portion of the Eastern Ghats, a chain of low interrupted ranges that sweep northeast in the direction of Chennai.

The Western Ghats have an average elevation of 915 m and are covered with tropical, temperate evergreen and mixed deciduous forest. The Malabar Coast forms a sedimentary plain into which are etched the waterways and lagoons that characterise Kerala.

Climate

The seasons in South India are distinctly wet and dry but do not show considerable variations in temperature as in North India. On the coast of Kerala, the average mean temperature varies no more than a few degrees. In the higher regions of the Western Ghats the climate is rather more temperate. One can enjoy a respite from the heat and humidity of the coast during the hottest months, in Ooty and Kodaikanal.

The southwest monsoon strikes Kerala first and drenches the state as it advances eastward from the Arabian Sea. It cools and soaks the windward slopes, as it rises over the Western Ghats. Within about 10 days the monsoon travels as far as northern Maharashtra and by early July it covers the entire country. The retreating monsoon blows in from the Bay of Bengal in November and early December and showers occur in Tamil Nadu and Kerala. Sometimes cyclones hit the coasts of Andhra Pradesh and Tamil Nadu. South India never presents any extreme weather conditions like hot summers or freezing winters that one encounters in many parts of North India.

Tamil Nadu

Tamil Nadu has a rich cultural heritage and it is believed that it has enjoyed the longest continuous habitation in India. A rich history, sculptural beauty, immaculate precision in architectural excellence, dance forms, music, religious rituals and the numerous customs and traditions reflected in the life of Tamilians make this state the heart of Dravidian culture. It is believed that once the Dravidians were spread over the whole of India and were the architects of the Indus Valley civilization of the 4th millennium BC. When the Aryans arrived in North India the Dravidians were pushed towards the south.

The ancient history of Tamil Nadu reveals many interesting facts. The Dravidian land was ruled by three dynasties, Chola, Pandya and Chera from the 4th century BC. The Cholas held supremacy in the present Thanjavur and Tiruchirapalli districts. They threatened the local people with military strength. Elara, a Chola Prince went ahead with his plan to expand his kingdom ad conquered Ceylon in the 2nd century BC. The Pandyas devoted much of their time towards learning and establishing trade relations with traders in and outside their kingdom.

The districts of Madurai and Thirunelveli and part of south Kerala came under their control. The Roman Emperor Augustus warmly received an ambassador sent by a Pandiyan king in the 1st century BC

The Pallavas of Kanchi remained in power and established their supremacy and regal splendour in the south for a period of 400 years between the 5th and 8th centuries AD. They subjugated the Chola dominions and took their armies even to Ceylon (Sri Lanka) in the 6th century. During the Pallava era the famous Alvars and Nayanars (sage poets) flourished and they brought about a spiritual awakening in the minds of the people. The Cholas became a great power in the south in the 9th century AD when they defeated the last of the Pallavas.

The Pandyas became dominant in the 13th century. Channels of international trade were established during their rule. The prosperity of Vijayanagar Empire brought about the downfall of the Pandyas. Soon Vijayanagar absorbed almost all the territories of the Pandyas. After the disintegration of the Vijayanagar Empire several petty kings apportioned Tamil Nadu among themselves.

Madras state was renamed as Tamil Nadu in August 1968. As the name suggests people of Tamil Nadu consider Tamil as a language enriched with all the qualities of an ancient culture and traditions. Among the Dravidian languages Sanskrit least influences Tamil. The earliest extant literature of the Tamils is called Sangam literature and it is dated between 500 BC and 200 AD. Tiruvalluvar's Tirukkural is acclaimed to be the greatest Tamil Classic. Tamil has produced two epics Silappadhikaram and Manimekhalai in the 3rd century. In the period between 13 and 18 century AD the works of Muslim and Christian writers influenced Tamil literature. The Christian influence began with the Portuguese and continued with the Dutch, the French and the British. The Italian priest Beschi composed the magnificent poetical work Tembavani on the life of St. Joseph.

1. *A rich and abundant paddy harvest in full swing*
2. *Women farmhands, something to smile about after a hard day's work*
3. *His moustache is his pride and joy*
4. *Technology and tradition in harmony*

1 2

General Information

Area, 130,000 sq km; Capital, Chennai (Madras); Population, 60 million; Language, Tamil; Literacy, M 75% F 52%; Best time to visit, November to February; Airports, Chennai, Tiruchirapalli, Coimbatore & Madurai.

The Geography

Tamil Nadu is the 11th largest state in India occupying 4% of the country's total area. Formerly known as the Coromandel Coast, it is bound on the east by the Bay of Bengal, in the South by the Indian Ocean in the west by the Arabian Sea and the states of Kerala and Karnataka and in the north by Karnataka and Andhra Pradesh.

The eastern coastal plain and the hilly region along the north and the west constitute the two natural divisions of Tamil Nadu. The hot, dry and dusty plains, the flat coast with alluvial soil and deltas at the mouths of major rivers make the habitat of this state unique and ineradicable.

The Western Ghats, averaging 1220 m above sea level and rising to 2440 m at its highest point runs along the western edge of the Deccan plateau. It runs approximately 1600 km through the states of Maharashtra, Goa, Kerala, Tamil Nadu and Karnataka. The only break in the great mountain wall is the Palghat Gap, about 25 km wide. The range is known as Anamalai or Elephant Hills to the south, and is known as the Nilgiris to the north. The famous hill station of Ootacamund or Ooty is in the Nilgiris. Doddabetta, the second highest peak in South India- rises 2640 m above sea level. The Palani Hills are in the east where the famous hill station of Kodaikanal is situated.

Nearly 18% of the area of Tamil Nadu is under forests. Dry deciduous, forests, thorn forests, scrub, mangroves and wetlands cover most of the plains and lower hills. Sandalwood, pulpwood, rubber and bamboo are important forest products.

Excepting the hills, Tamil Nadu's climate can be classified as tropical with little variaton between the summer and winter temperatures. The hottest months are from April to June. Maximum temperatures in the plains could be as high as 45°C in summer with the minimum temperatures in the winter hovering around 10°C. The monsoon is active over Tamil Nadu from October to December. The average annual rainfall ranges between 650 and 1900 mm.

Wildlife found in the state includes elephant, tiger, leopard, striped hyena, jackals, Indian pangolin, slender loris, lion tailed macaque, sloth bear, bison or gaur, black buck, Nilgiris tatur, grizzled giant squirrel, dugong and mouse deer.

Tamil Nadu is sometimes called a land of temples. The state has more than 30,000 temples. Suchindram, Rameswaram, Tiruchendur, Madurai, Palani, Tiruchirapalli, Srirangam, Thanjavur, Kumbakonam, Nagore, Velankanni, Vaitheeswaram Koil, Chidambaram, Tiruvannamalai, Kanchipuram, Tiruttani and Kanyakumari are the famous religious places in Tamil Nadu.

1. *A rickshaw puller patiently waits for a customer*
2. *Harnessing the sea for salt, Tuticorin produces about 25 per cent of India's salt*
3. *Traditional farming methods are still used extensively*
4. *A goatherd watches as the goats devour all things green*
5. *A colourful wedding procession*

Festivals

There are festivals here through out the year. Prominent festivals and fairs celebrated in Tamil Nadu are Pongal, Chittirai Festival, Navarathri, Saral Vizha, Kanthur Festival, Mahamagam Festival, Thyagaraja Festival and Mahabalipuram Dance Festival. A few of the prominent amongst them are listed below.

January: Pongal (Harvest Festival), state-wide; Film Festival, Chennai; Tourist & Trade Fare, Chennai; Saral Vizha, Courtallam; Mahabalipuram Dance Festival, Mahabalipuram; Temple Car Festival, Kanchipuram; Temple Car Festival, Tiruchirapalli; Thaipusam Festival, Palani; Thyagaraja Music Festival, Thiruvaiyaru.

January/February: Teppam (Float) Festival, Madurai; Crafts Mela, Mahabalipuram; Maha Shivarathri, Kanchipuram & Rameswaram.

February: Natyanjali Dance Festival, Chidambaram; Feast of Our Lady of Lourdes, Tiruchirapalli; Perur Temple Festival, Coimbatore.

1. A proud farmer admires his golden crop
2. Paddy planting in progress
3. A woman decorates the entrance of her house
4. Kolam, intricate and geometric patterns created with rice flour
5. Looking towards a bright future
6. The face of spiritual India
7. A Brahmin watches the world go by

February/March: Masi Magham, Swami Malai.

April/May: Temple Car Festival, Chidambaram & Kanchipuram; Chithirai, state-wide.

May/June: Kumari Amman Temple Festival, Kanyakumari; Flower Show, Ooty; Kavadi Festival, Palani

July/August: Drowpathiamman Temple Festival of Fire, Pondicherry; Adi Pooram, Madurai & Srivilliputtur.

September: Feast of Our Lady of Good Health, Velanganni; Avanimoolam, Madurai.

October: Navarathri, state-wide.

November/December: Karthikai Deepam Festival, Thiruvannamalai & Swamimalai.

December: Vaikunta Ekadasi (Paradise Festival), Tiruchirapalli.

December/January: Temple Car Festival, Chidambaram; Music & Dance Festival, Chennai.

1

Mahabalipuram

History finds its full display in the marvellous sculptures of the temples in Mahabalipuram.

The place derived its name from Narasimha Varman I who was also known as Mahamalla the great wrestler. When we trace back the various tides and triumphs in the tumultuous life of Pallava kings we find that the Tamil dynasty was at the height of its political power and artistic creativity between the 5th and 8th centuries AD.

Mahabalipuram is now famous for its spectacular Shore Temple. It has now become a UNESCO World Heritage site. Once it was a thriving port of the Pallava empire.

Just stand on the shores enjoying the cool breeze and you can watch the waves thrashing against the wall of the Shore Temple surrounded by rows of Nandi bulls eagerly looking out to sea. Most of the temples and rock carvings here were completed during the reigns of Narasimha Varman I and Narasimha Varman II.

If you were to make a list of the most photographed monuments in India, the Shore Temple would definitely

1

2

appear in it. The sculpture here is fascinating because it shows scenes of day-to-day life: women milking buffaloes, ostentatious lords moving around the kingdom, young maidens with wide open eyes, their faces displaying the ebullience of youthful vigour posing provocatively at street corners. In many temples through out the state you would find carvings of gods and goddesses mostly and you can't expect ordinary folks meddling with ethereal beings.

Chisel and stone have not yet disappeared from Mahabalipuram. Stone carving is still a living craft in this place. As you move through the streets you can meet a number of sculptors diligently engaged in stone carving. Indeed Mahabalipuram has now become famous for its sculptors. This pleasant little village is positioned at the foot of a low-lying boulder-strewn hill.

The Shore Temple's two main spires house shrines for Shiva. A third and earlier shrine is dedicated to Vishnu and has his reclining image.

The five Rathas (chariots): Draupadi Ratha, Arjuna Ratha, Bhima Ratha, Dharmaraja Ratha and the Nakula–Sahadeva Ratha are sculptured temples in the style of chariots. As their names suggest these Rathas depict important incidents in the lives of Pandava brothers and heroes of Mahabharata. Mahabalipuram unfolds the pages of history and mythology through the marvellous carvings and perspicuous sculptural beauty reflecting the immaculate precision in visualisation and design that eminent craftsmen had in the period between 5th and 8th century.

If you undertake a journey from Mahabalipuram towards the north you would reach Tiger Cave, a rock-cut shrine dedicated to Durga.

Mahabalipuram Dance Festival starts in early January and lasts for 4 weeks. Dance forms from all over India are staged here usually in the open air, with Arjuna's Penance forming a magnificent backdrop.

Previous page

1.Arjuna's penance sculpted in rock

2.Standing tall and majestic, the Shore Temple at Mahabalipuram

1. Mahabalipuram Dance Festival, Arjuna's penance forms a magnificent backdrop

2. The lighthouse Mahabalipuram

3. In anticipation of a good day's business on the beach

1

2

Kanchipuram

Kanchipuram is one of India's most spectacular temple cities and its many gopurams (pyramids) can be seen from miles away. Situated just 76 km west of Chennai, it is one of the seven sacred cities of India. Unlike other cities, which are usually dedicated to either Lord Vishnu or Lord Shiva, Kanchipuram is dedicated to both and is also the most important city dedicated to Goddess Kamakshi (Durga).

Once Kanchipuram was a sophisticated city with diverse cultures and languages. It was a major Buddhist centre established by the Mauryan emperor Ashoka in about the 3rd century.

The temple car festivals in the months of January, April and May attract many tourists and pilgrims to Kanchipuram.

The oldest and the most beautiful temple in Kanchipuram is the Kailashnatha Temple dedicated to Lord Shiva and built of honey-coloured sandstone. Built by the Pallava ruler Rayasimha, in the late 7th century AD, the temple has 58 small shrines built around it. Sri Ekambaranath Temple is also dedicated to Lord Shiva and is one of the largest in Kanchipuram, covering an area of over 12 hectares. It has a 59 m tall gopuram and was constructed in the 16th century AD by the Vijayanagar kings. In one of the enclosures of the temple is a mango tree believed to be over 3000 years old.

Kamakshi Amman Temple is dedicated to the goddess Parvati in her guise as Kamakshi. Visitors offer precious gifts to the goddess in the hope of having their prayers answered.

Vardarajaperumal Temple is an enormous monument with a massive outer wall and a 100-pillared hall within itself. It is dedicated to Lord Vishnu. The 100 -pillared hall is a perfect specimen of Vijayanagara art and architecture. One of its most notable sculptural marvels is a huge chain carved out of a single piece of stone.

1. Vardarajaperumal Temple, the highlight of Vishnu Kanchi built on top of Hastagiri Hill

2. Shankaracharya's ashram in Kanchipuram boasts of an unbroken line of 70 acharyas (spiritual leaders)

3. Vardarajaperumal Temple Kanchipuram The 100–pillared hall is a splendid specimen of Vijayanagar art and architecture

3

Kanchipuram Silks

Kanchi silks are of the highest quality in India and intricate designs make them unique creations of art. Silk and cotton weaving industries produce a variety of dress materials and you can find the weavers fully involved in the careful craft of weaving. We cannot easily trace back the period when the weavers first came to Kanchee. It is believed that they arrived in the 12th century. Another story talks about Krishna Devaraya and his desire to develop the art of weaving. He probably might have invited the weavers to settle down in Kanchipuram to do their job. In the beginning only vegetable dyes were used to colour the thread. Nowdays weavers depend on chemical dyes to make charming colour combinations. The narrow lanes in Kanchipuram are inhabited by the silk merchants. Slowly various steps in the weaving process will be revealed to you if you stand watching the looms and the men who operate them with utmost care and concern.

1. *Silky magic! A weaver weaving an intricate pattern in silk*
2. *Gingee fort, one of the few forts to survive in Tamil Nadu*
3. *The majestic Shiva Temple built by the Cholas is now in ruins*
4. *It is time this relic was renovated*
5. *The majestic gopurams on Temple Street in Kanchipuram*
6. *A Kanchipuram silk sari, no wardrobe is complete without one*

Gingee

Gingee is the site of an extensive fort complex set in a silent and serene landscape. Every nook and corner of this structure reveals history in its myriad forms of events, conflicts and fierce battles. During the period of the Vijayanagar Empire, the fort was occupied by various armies, including the forces of Adil Shah from Bijapur.

In 1648 he renamed the complex as Badshabad. The Marathas took control of the fort in 1677. Later on The Mughals occupied it and in the middle of the 18th century the French took possession of the fort. The British held it under their control till the turn of the 19th century.

The dilapidated structure certainly has a special charm. The curious traveller can spend an entire day here. Among the relics you would find a granary, a Shiva temple and a mosque offering you a mysterious harmony of religious beliefs and annihilation. The prominent building Kalyana Mahal contains a pagoda-like structure which was used for wedding ceremonies. Stepping into the this great citadel is indeed an unusual experience.

The fort is constructed on three separate hills. You would find Krishnagiri to the north Chandrayan Durg to the south and Rajagiri to the east.

The fortified walls extend to a length of 5 km and are 15 m thick at some places. Through out the complex there are a number of horse and elephant stables which certainly would not escape your attention. Rajagiri hill is 165 m high and climbing it could be a strenuous affair. You can easily reach the top of Krishnagiri without utilising your precious energy. The fort and its surroundings have certain features that attract the film producers. A number of films have used this dramatic location to produce blockbusters. This silent landscape may appear like a surrealistic painting as many things are merged in its surroundings like strokes of brush on a canvas.

1 2 3

Pondicherry

Pondicherry (or Puducherry as it is called today) was a former French colony. Pondicherry became a French colony in 1675, but Anglo–French conflicts for Pondicherry lasted nearly 300 years. In 1954 the French voluntarily handed over Pondicherry along with the other colonies of Karaikal (Tamil Nadu), Mahé (Kerala) and Yanam (Andhra Pradesh) to the Indian Government. Pondicherry is now a Union Territory.

Pondicherry is indeed a beautiful Indian town with traces of French culture still intact and an ashram by the sea. Although there are plenty of reminders of its colonial past including the distinct uniform of the Police, the imposing French Consulate, the occasional French being spoken on the streets and French influence on the local cuisine, Pondicherry is essentially an Indian city–just a little bit more easy going and cleaner!

Archaeologists believe that there were two ancient colonies here, Vedapuri and Podhigal. Vedapuri was where scholars studied the Vedas or ancient Hindu texts and Podhigal was where the sage Agastya set up his hermitage in 1500 BC. Recent excavations near Pondicherry have revealed that it had significant trade relations with ancient Greece and Rome around the 1st century AD.

Sri Aurobindo (1872–1950) founded Sri Aurobindo Ashram. Aurobindo was a Bengali revolutionary and philosopher who fought against the British and wanted to free India from the shackles of colonization. Following his imprisonment, he left Calcutta in 1910 and arrived at Pondicherry where the French welcomed him. He started the ashram to put into practice his ideals of a peaceful community brought together ingeniously by combining yogic philosophy with modern science. Following his death his activities were continued by his favourite lifetime companion and French disciple universally referred to as the Mother.

The Mother passed away in 1973 at the age of 97.

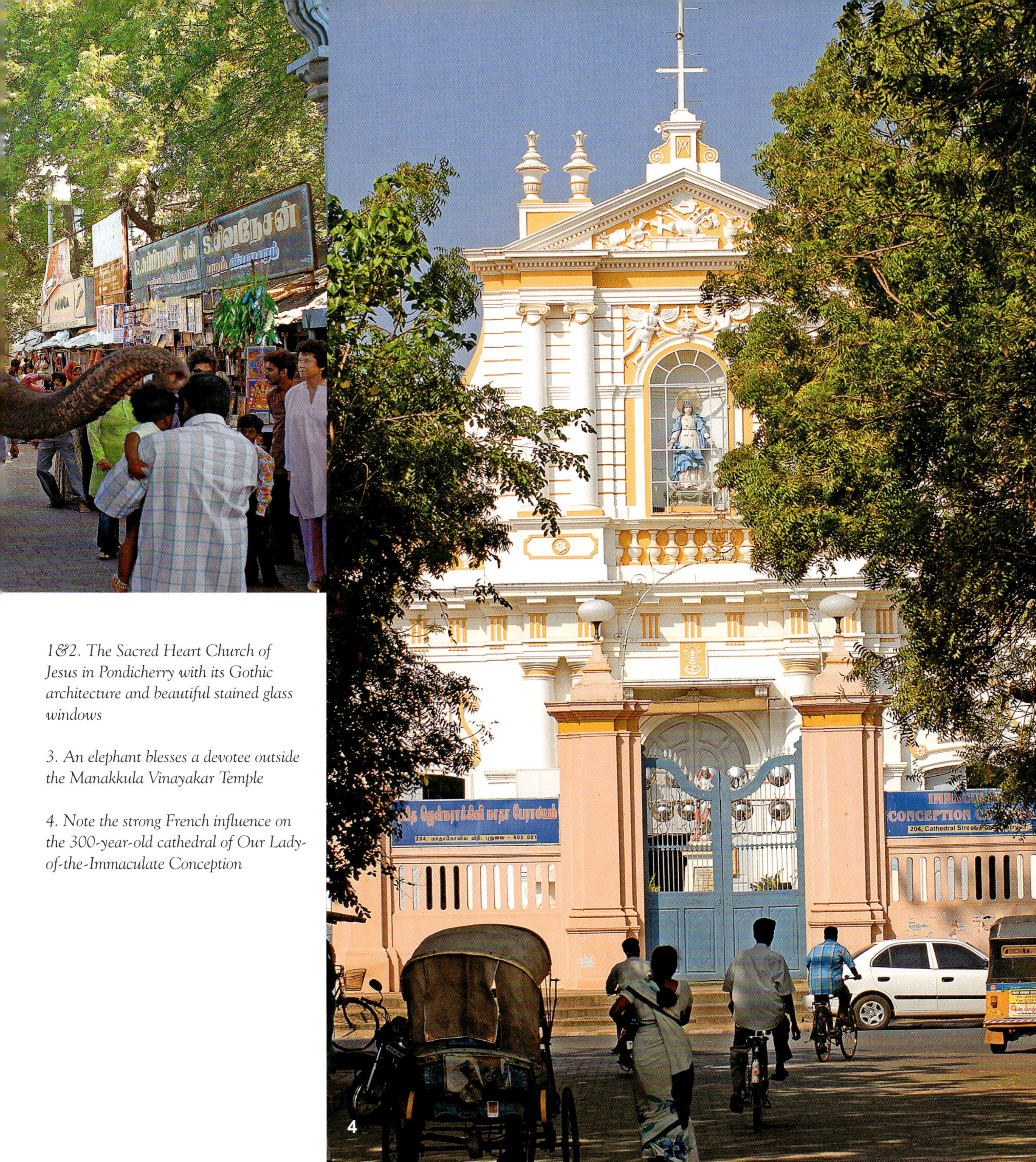

1&2. The Sacred Heart Church of Jesus in Pondicherry with its Gothic architecture and beautiful stained glass windows

3. An elephant blesses a devotee outside the Manakkula Vinayakar Temple

4. Note the strong French influence on the 300-year-old cathedral of Our Lady-of-the-Immaculate Conception

The ashram continues to promote a lot of educational and cultural activities at Pondicherry. This ashram is now one of the most popular and affluent establishments and attracts a lot of Western visitors.

The Sri Aurobindo Handmade Paper Factory is a successful ashram enterprise; it is more an artist's workshop than a paper factory. The paper produced here is exported to many countries and a wide range of products is available at the sales office. The factory is on SV Patel Road, and is open on all weekdays except Sunday. The keen tourist could watch paper being made in this factory

North of Pondicherry on the Tamil Nadu border is Auroville, the brainchild of the Mother designed by a French architect Roger Arger. Conceived as an experiment in international living, men and women live here in perfect harmony with each other regardless of nationality, creed and politics, symbolising universal oneness. The project has over 1200 residents including children and

1. *A quiet street in Pondicherry's French quarter*
2. *The Mahatma watches over the city of Pondicherry*
3. *A policeman in his red 'kepi'*
4. *A vendor waiting in hope.*
5. *The war memorial, built by the French dedicated to the soldiers who died in World War 1*
6. *Gazing at the tranquil blue waters of the Bay of Bengal*

they are all involved in various specialised fields of work. The Mathamandir is the spiritual and physical centre of Auroville.

The Pondicherry Museum has a good collection of sculptures and an interesting section on the recent archaeological findings connecting Pondicherry with ancient Rome and Greece apart from a superb collection of snail shells from around Pondicherry.

The 1500 m long beach that borders the town on the eastern side is clean and is ideal for swimming and sun bathing.

There are a number of churches and temples that are worth visiting here. The Church of the Sacred Heart of Jesus located on South Boulevard is built in the Gothic style and is one of the most beautiful churches in the city. The Manakkula Vinayakar Temple dedicated to lord Ganesha and Vardaraja Temple where Vishnu is the main deity are definitely worth a visit.

Chidambaram

Chidambaram is situated 60 km south of Pondicherry, and about 245 km away from Chennai. The Nataraja Temple, depicting the cosmic dance of Lord Shiva, is the star attraction of this temple town. This temple is home to Chidambara Rahasyam, where Lord Shiva is worshipped in his 'formless form' (Aroopam).

The Nataraja Temple is set within a walled rectangular frame, and covers an area of about 22 hectares. Of the four gopurams surrounding it, the north and south ones are 49 m tall, with seven tiers. The long, awesome corridors surrounding the sanctum contain sculptured pillared halls and numerous shrines.

Once the capital of the erstwhile Cholas from 907–1310 AD, Chidambaram is 9 km north of the Kollidam River (Coleroon in English), which is the northern limit of the Cauvery delta and is one of the most important holy towns in Tamil Nadu.

1. A priest inside the Nataraja temple at Chidambaram
2. A view of one of the halls at Airateswara temple in Darusaram
3&5. A glimpse of the brilliant sculptures that adorn the walls of the Airateswara temple
4. The majestic and colourful gopuram of the Nataraja temple, Chidambaram decorated with miniature shrines

Darasuram

The grandeur of Chola architecture is at its full display in Airateswara or Darasuram Temple built by Raja Raja Chola ll in the 12th century AD. This well presented temple is slightly off the tourist trail but is well worth a visit. The musical stone stairs that produce metallic notes when struck, the Maha Mandapam (grand hall) and the unique miniature sculptures on the columns set this temple in a class by itself. The large stone statues surrounding the temple were replaced with brick and mortar statues similar to those found at the big temple in Thanjavur

UNESCO has declared Darasuram Temple a world heritage site. The temple was restored recently and is being maintained by the archaeological survey of India.

Gangaikondacholapuram

Gangaikondacholapuram or 'the town of the Chola who conquered/brought the Ganga' is about 60 km North of Thanjavur. The Brihadishwara temple at Gangaikondacholapuram was conceived and constructed by the Chola King Rajendra 1 son of Raja Raja Cholan who built the Brihadishwara Temple of Thanjavur. Rajendra 1 built this temple after his victory over the kingdoms bordering the river Ganga. The sculptures here are as magnificent as in any other Chola temple. Apart from the huge Nandi, there are some beautiful sculptures including a dancing Ganesha, a lion-headed well and a stunning frieze depicting Rajendra being crowned by Shiva and Parvathi. Perhaps the most striking of all is Ardhanari (the man–woman manifestation of Lord Shiva). Ardhanari is supposed to represent the synthesis of male and female energies.

1. The majestic Nandi at the Gangaikondacholapuram Shiva Temple, built by the Chola emperor Rajendra I

2. A shrine on a hillock, Swamimalai (God's mountain) Temple dedicated to Lord Muruga

3. Mendicants on the steps of Lord Muruga's Temple at Swamimalai

4. A shop selling flowers, coconuts and bananas which are offered to the Lord during puja (worship)

5. A humble devotee on his way to see lord Shiva at the Brihadiswara Temple at Gangaikondacholapuram

6. Acclaimed as one of the finest metal workers in the world, the artisans in Swamimalai have built this bronze chariot

1

Thanjavur

Thanjavur (also popularly known as Tanjore) was once the capital of the Chola dynasty and later of the Thanjavur Nayak and Maratha rulers. The Cholas built most of the 93 odd temples here. Although they were great patrons of art and lavished their wealth on building temples, they also encouraged the practice of donating part of one's wealth to the temples for spiritual gain. Set in a fertile delta, agriculture is a major industry here. Thanjavur is also famous for its silk, carpets, jewellery and musical instruments.

One of the greatest Chola rulers was Raja Raja (985–1014 AD), who built the Brihadishwara Temple, Thanjavur's main attraction. His son Rajendra I (1014–1044 AD) fought the Arabs for control over trade routes in the Indian Ocean.

The Brihadishwara Temple, also known as the 'Big Temple', is a World Heritage Monument. This temple dedicated to Lord Shiva is set in spacious grounds and has several pillared halls and shrines. The monolithic granite block on top of the tower weighing an astounding 82 tonnes was lifted up and put in place in a manner similar to the way the Egyptians lifted blocks to build their pyramids.

The gateway to the inner courtyard is guarded by a gigantic Nandi (the bull, Shiva's vehicle) second only to the largest one at the Lepakshi temple in Andhra Pradesh. Created from a single piece of rock, it weighs 25 tonnes!

1. *Brihadiswara Temple, Thanjavur. A view of the gopuram and the dominating monolithic granite block on top of it*
2. *A girl waiting to offer a lotus flower to Lord Shiva*
3. *The spacious and well-maintained grounds surrounding the Brihadiswara Temple at Thanjavur*

Tiruchirapalli

Situated 55 km from Thanjavur at the head of the Cauvery delta is the ancient town of Tiruchirapalli often referred to as Trichy or Tiruchy for short. Once a bastion of the Chola dynasty centuries before Christ, it gained eminence under the Nayaks of Madurai, who built the fort and temple. It changed hands many a time and was with the Vijayanagar Emperors until their defeat by the Deccan Sultans in the 16th century.

Trichy's landmark monument is the Rock Fort from where the wars of the Carnatic were waged in the 18th century during the British–French struggle for domination in India.

Rock Fort Temple is a spectacular monument perched 83 m high on a rocky out growth rising abruptly from the surrounding plains in the centre of the town. The Nayaks of Madurai used its naturally fortified position to their advantage at times of battle. The Vinayaka Temple at the summit is dedicated to Lord Ganesha. Although the climb is tough, the view is stunning and makes the trouble well worth the effort. There are several small shrines along the way up on this smooth rock face and the remains of a 1000-pillared hall destroyed in the 18th century. Further up at the end of the last flight of steps is the Sri Thayumanaswami Temple dedicated to Lord Shiva.

1. *Rock fort Temple at Trichy sits atop a hill and dedicated to lord Ganesha*

2. *Sadhus waiting for alms from generous passers by*

3. *Sri Ranganathaswamy Temple at Srirangam is 236 ft.- high with 13 tiers and is believed to be the tallest temple tower in Asia*

Ooty

Ooty was the first established hill station in India and is considered the 'Queen of the Blue Mountains'. The British founded this popular hill station in the early 19th century as the summer capital of the Madras government. Prior to this, the Toda tribal people inhabited it and their way of life centred on the buffalo. Today only about 1500 of them remain and you see their shrines in various places throughout the hills.

In spite of the influx of hoteliers and real estate developers who have literally changed the topography of this once beautiful laid back town, one can still see remnants of the British occupation in the single-storey stone cottages, winding lanes with tall leafy eucalyptus, the stone churches, the private schools and the Ooty Club House. The Maharaja's summer palace harks back to yet another era.

1. The beautiful green fields that adorn the undulating Nilgiri hills

2. The British built St. Thomas church overlooking the picturesque lake in the late 19th century

3. A traditional Toda house. Note the unique oval shape of the dwelling

4. Fernhill Palace in Ooty was a summer resort for the British during the Raj

5. Row upon row of cauliflower ready to be harvested

6. Two young girls smile shyly for the camera

Mudumalai

Mudumalai Wildlife Sanctuary & National Park is situated at the trifurcation of the three southern states of Tamil Nadu, Karnataka and Kerala. This 322 sq km of tropical wilderness is part of the 'Nilgiri Biosphere Reserve'. It was established in 1932 and was the first to be declared a national park. Easily accessible from both Ooty and Mysore, this place is a favourite among day-trippers who often unfortunately destroy the tranquillity.

Mudumalai, which means 'Ancient Hills', comprises mostly of tropical dry and moist deciduous forests with some secondary grasslands, swamps, bamboo, sandalwood and teak. Perhaps the largest number of wild and domesticated elephants in South India is found here. You could also spot Gaur, deer (spotted, barking and Sambar), wild dogs, giant squirrels, sloth bear, leopards and pangolins.

With over 200 species of sedentary and migratory birds, Mudumalai has a fascinating miscellany of birds and is indeed a bird-watcher's paradise. These include the golden oriole, paradise fly catcher, Malabar grey hornbill, scarlet minivet, golden-backed woodpecker, king fishers, peacocks, parakeets, rare sirkeer cuckoos and speckled peculates. Otters and crocodiles inhabit the Moyar River that flows through the park and separates it from the Bandipur National Park in Karnataka.

1. Elephants roam freely at the Mudumlai wildlife sanctuary

2. A female Gaur (Indian Bison) takes stock of her surroundings

3&4. The hilly terrain and luscious and varied vegetation make Mudumalai an ideal wildlife sanctuary

5. Machans (platforms built on trees) in Mudumalai reserve are the perfect way to observe wildlife

1

2

Chettinad

Chettinad is the land of the Chettiars or the Nagarathars (townsfolk), as they would prefer to be called. The Chettiars are a merchant community blessed with a rare financial acumen and an inborn talent for trade. These traits have helped them travel and settle in different parts of the globe and in the process they have created a rich and vivid history.

Legend has it that the Chettiars played a pivotal role in the business world of the Chola Empire. They are said to have dominated the coastal business as gem dealers, ship-chandlers and salt merchants. Respected by the rulers and successful in business, they established links across the seas. It was smooth sailing for the Chettiars, until the king abducted a Chettiar girl to make her his wife. The Chettiar community strongly believed in the sanctity of marriage within the community and retaliated to this treacherous act of the monarch. There are many legends as to what happened after this event. But whatever be the legend, the Chettiars seem to have migrated to the Pandya Kingdom in the 13th century AD and settled in four villages around a temple in the village of Ilayathangudi, about 25 km west of Karaikudi (the most important town of Chettinad).

As the community grew larger, the Chettiars established about 96 villages and new temples. Of all the temples, nine Shiva Temples have become an integral part of the Nagarathar lineage. They are Illyathangudi, Mathur, Vairavanpatti, Iraniyur, Pillaiyarpatti, Namam, Iluppakudi, Soorakudi, and Velangudi. Every Chettiar, irrespective of his place of birth, is born a member of one of the nine temples to which his father belongs.

It's amazing how the Chettiars reveled in a land that had nothing much to offer. Perhaps it's their inherent financial sense that urged them to trade rice from the rich Cauvery Delta and transport salt from the Coromandel Coast to the interiors of the Pandya and Chera kingdoms. They used their knowledge of diamonds and precious stones to establish trade in the orient. Business flourished. They accumulated wealth and created fortress-like mansions earning themselves the title Nattukotai (land-fort) Chettiars. They filled their homes with riches earned from across the seas, acquired land, built temples, Veda padasalas (religious institutions) and charitable hospitals. They earned their preferred community name—Nagarathar, the townsfolk or the people of the Nagarams (urban settlements), and rightly so.

For over 100 years, from the middle of the 19th century to the early 20th century, the Chettiars were a vital element of local finance and trade in several South and Southeast Asian countries which were then under the rule of either the British, French or Dutch.

The Chettiars also made significant contributions to the development of Ceylon, Burma, the Federated Malay States, Indochina and Sumatra, the Straits Settlements and Mauritius. But the joy of independence in Southeast Asia after World War II was the Chettiars' nemesis. Their trade was so badly affected that it turned out to be their darkest period in history. By then the 96 villages in Chettinad had shrunk to 75. However, education has been responsible for a considerable resurgence since the 1970s, with many members of the community becoming successful industrialists and professionals in South India and around the world.

The bounty the Nagarathar earned during their glorious yesteryears is evident even today in the palatial mansions, arts and crafts that embellish their homes and temples in Chettinad. They evoke the ancient traditions of a splendid past.

1. *A typical Chettinad house situated in Kanadukathan in Tamil Nadu, which has been declared a heritage town. Chettinad consists of 75 villages, each village consisting of a cluster of huge mansions, extending over 30 to 40 thousand sq. ft.*
2. *The owner of a grand house in Kanadukathan sitting in a swing in the well decorated front hall*
3. *An imposing front view of the Chettinad Palace in Kanadukathan*
4. *Chettinad Mansion, an architectural marvel, with a constructed area of 41000 sq. ft., built over 100 years back . Italian Marble, English steel, and Burmese Teak wood has been lavishly used. A heritage resort, popularly known as Chettinad Mansion is run in this palatcial building*
5. *Chandramouli, a retired high tech professional, and owner of Chettinad Mansion, with his wife Sivagami, sitting in a relaxed mood*
6. *A view of one of the 150-year-old palacial building under active consideration for becoming a monument*

Madurai

Madurai one of South India's most ancient cities is situated on the banks of the Vaigai River. Tamil and Greek literature record its existence from the 4th century BC. It has been the focus of learning and pilgrimage for centuries.

The Pandiyan rulers made Madurai their capital and ruled from here for four centuries until the 10th century AD when the Cholas took over briefly before handing it back to the Pandiyans who later lost it to the invading Muslims led by Malik Kaufer. In the 14th century the Hindu Vijayanagar kings of Hampi captured Madurai.

In the 16th century, the Nayaks took over and it was during the glorious reign of Tirumalai Nayak (1623–1655 AD) that Madurai became the cultural centre of the Tamils, playing a pivotal role in the development of the Tamil language.

1. The colossal Meenakshi Temple

2. In Goddess Meenakshi's service; priests inside the Temple's precincts

3. A young priest waits for his devotees

4. Devotees offering special prayers to the goddess

5. *Strands of fragrant jasmine for sale*

6. *Normal life on a Madurai street*

7. *The majestic gopuram adorned with brightly coloured figures*

The Meenakshi Temple in the heart of the old town is the supreme attraction here. This outstanding example of Dravidian architecture, although designed by Viswanatha Nayak in 1560, was built during the reign of Tirumalai Nayak. Dedicated to Goddess Meenakshi, protector of Madurai, the rectangular temple complex is almost a city within a city as all manner of business is conducted in this vast area spread over 350 hectares and enclosed by large walls. Each wall has a nine-storey high gopuram brightly coloured and decorated with thousands of celestial and animal figures. Within the walls the, long corridors lead to the gold covered sanctums of the deities.

Another attraction in Madurai is the Tirumalai Nayak Palace, which was built in the early 17th century in the Indo-Saracenic style of architecture and situated about 2 km away from the Meenakshi temple; it was once the proud possession of Tirumalai Nayak.

1

Kerala

Welcome to Kerala or the land of coconuts, as the name denotes. Kerala is a narrow strip of land situated in the southwestern tip of the Indian peninsula. This tropical paradise has been certified by the National Geographic Traveler as one of the 50 must-see places of a lifetime! The serene beaches, lush vegetation, stunning mountains, spice-perfumed air and an amiable culture that embraces Hinduism, Christianity, Islam, Jainism and Judaism gives Kerala its unique identity. Kerala is one of the most progressive and literate states in the country, yet an easy-going relaxed atmosphere prevails here.

Kerala is also home to Kathakali, Kalarippayat, Ayurveda, mesmerizing backwaters and houseboats. Kathakali derived from the Malayalam words Katha (story) and Kali (play) is a complex and ritualised dance drama based on the ancient Hindu epics. It originated in Kerala in the 17th century. One of the most interesting aspects of Kathakali is the make-up code. The dance was traditionally performed in temples but nowadays one can see theatre performances as well.

3

Kalarippayat (Kalari, an arena for combat; Payat, a system of combat) is a highly stylised martial art that originated in Kerala. Historians believe that it is perhaps one of the oldest forms of martial arts in the world. Kerala is also home to Ayurveda the primordial system of medicine that uses herbs and massage to treat a range of ailments. Ayurveda is acknowledged worldwide for both its scientific principles and treatment methods.

Kerala is a land of rivers and backwaters. Forty-four rivers criss-cross her with their innumerable tributaries and branches. The backwaters form a specially attractive and valuable feature of Kerala. They include lakes and ocean inlets, which stretch irregularly along the coast. The deltas of the rivers interlink the backwaters and provide excellent water transportation in the lowlands. A navigable canal, 367 km long, extends from Trivandrum the capital city in the south to Tirur in the north. The waterways of Kerala have played an important role in the economy of the state. Rice boats and small ships used to ply in these waters, carrying coconut, rubber, rice and spices to various trading centres of Kerala. Even today, these waterways link remote villages and islands with the main land. It is an incredibly different experience to cruise in the backwaters in country boats, absorbing the beauty of the villages.

1. *A traffic jam of sorts!*
2. *A beautiful Kerala girl–untouched by life's worries*
3. *Sivan Vesham. A Kathakali dancer in elaborate Vesham (make-up) portrays the character of Lord Shiva*
4. *Fishing in the picturesque backwaters of Kerala*
5. *Fishermen get ready to go to sea*
6. *The rolling tea gardens of Kerala*
7. *East Fort Gate (Kizhakke Kotta Vathil) in Trivandrum. The fort is built around the famous Padmanabhaswamy Temple*

The traditional houseboat of Kerala is one of the most enduring images of the backwaters. These houseboats are converted forms of the 'Kuttanadan Kettuvallams'. They are comfortably furnished and offer adequate accommodation for a whole family, with a sitting room, a bedroom and a kitchen. These palm covered country boats were designed to carry cargo, such as coconut and spices, and to provide living accommodation for the boatmen.

General Information

Area: 38,863 sq. km; Capital: Thiruvananthapuram (Trivandrum as it is more popularly known); Population: 34 million; Language: Malayalam; Literacy: 100%; Best time to visit: October to March; Airports: Trivandrum, Kochi & Kozhikode.

The Geography

Kerala is bordered by the Arabian Sea to the west and the Western Ghats to the east and can be divided into three geographical regions: Highlands, Midlands and Lowlands. The Highlands slope down from the Western Ghats which rise to an average height of 900 m, with a number of peaks well over 1800 m high. This region is a favourite among tourists as it enjoys a cool and invigorating climate the year-round. Plantation crops including coffee, tea, rubber, cardamom and other spices are cultivated here. The Midlands, lying between the mountains and the lowlands, is made up of undulating hills and valleys. This is an area of intense cultivation. Cashew, coconut, areca nut, tapioca, banana, rice, pepper, sugar cane and different varieties of vegetables are grown in this area. The Lowlands or the coastal area is made up of river deltas, backwaters and the Arabian Sea and is essentially a land of coconuts and rice.

1. A crimson sunset on the Arabian Sea
2. An elephant ride on the beach, all part of the outing
3. A statue of Lord Nataraja for sale
4. 'Don't mess with me' says this tusker!
5. Kerala has several old and majestic churches
6. Skilled hands picking tender tea leaves

Kovalam

One of Kerala's most popular beach resorts, Kovalam, is situated just 15 km from Trivandrum city centre. Thirty years ago it was a picture-perfect tropical beach; a traditional fishing village and a favourite hangout for mellow backpackers. Today this tiny beach on the Arabian Sea consisting of two palm-fringed coves (Lighthouse Beach & Hawah Beach) separated from the less-populated north and south by rocky headlands, is the centre of a multi-million dollar business. Thousands of tourists from Britain and Europe come here on chartered flights for a quick fix of sun, sand and a rather sanitised Indian experience. Despite this influx of tourists this idyllic beach is still surprisingly safe and clean. Local fishermen still sail their boats out to sea each night and watching them haul in their nets early in the mornings is indeed a fascinating sight.

1. Fishermen examine their rather disappointing haul

2. The Arabian Sea at dawn

3. A young boy smiles shyly at the camera

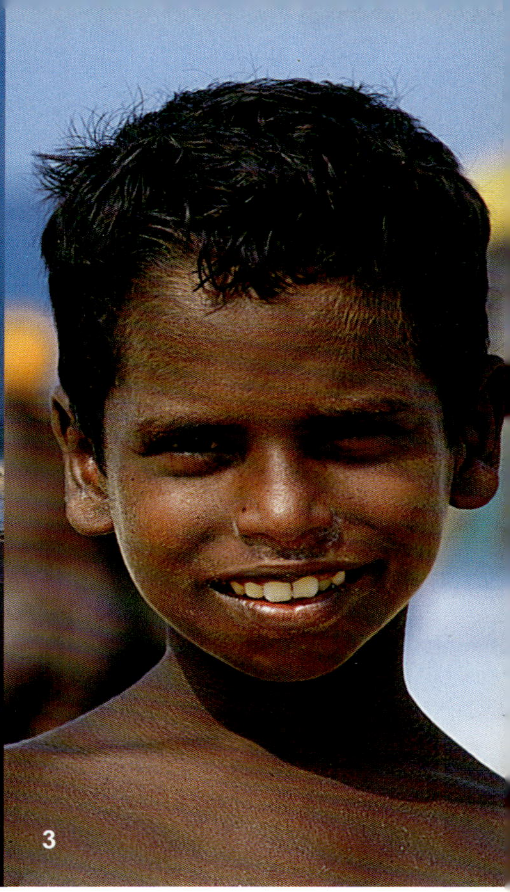

4. *Tourists relaxing on Kovalam beach against a picturesque back drop*

5. *The towering gopuram of the sprawling Sri Padmanabhaswamy Temple in Trivandrum*

Trivandrum

Trivandrum (now known officially as Thiruvananthapuram) is built over seven hills and is situated on the southern tip of Kerala. Known as the 'City of the Sacred Serpent', Trivandrum derives its name from Anantha, the serpent upon which the deity of the city, Padmanabha, an incarnation of Lord Vishnu, reclines. The Sri Padmanabha Swamy Temple is a landmark of the city.

In spite of its growth as a cosmopolitan capital city complete with political slogans, posters and protest marches, Trivandrum has managed to retain some of the ambience characteristic of old Kerala like red-tiled roofs and Nalukettu or rambling old ancestral homes with an open courtyard in the centre. But links to the past and an easy-going way of life are fast disappearing with widening of roads and construction of multi-storeyed apartments and shopping malls around the city.

Varkala

Forty-one kilometres north of Trivandrum is Varkala. Varkala is primarily a temple town with a sacred beach, but it is fast developing as a popular beach resort. There are mineral water springs on the towering reddish cliffs and the beach below is excellent for sunbathing and unwinding. An Arabian Sea sunset viewed from atop the cliff is truly magnificent. The town and train station are 2 km from the beach.

The attractive south Kerala style Janardhana Temple at the head of the beach is an important centre of pilgrimage. It is off limits to Non-Hindus although you can wander around the temple grounds. The Shivagiri Mutt, a hill in Varkala village is the headquarters of Sree Narayana Dharma Sanghom Trust. This ashram is devoted to Sree Narayana Guru (1855–1928) who preached unity of mankind through the principle of 'one caste, one religion, and one god for man' and was revered by the lower castes.

1. *Fishing boats in Kollam raring to venture out to sea*
2. *Wonder what he is thinking about!*
3. *Spectators enjoying the bullock race at Ananthapalli, in Kollam district*

4. *Relaxing on a clean and quiet beach in Varkala*

5. *The Kettukazhcha festival at the Chettikulangara Bhagvathy Temple in Alleppey Dist. Tall chariots on wheeled platforms, brightly decorated effigies of horses and bullocks and cultural performances mark the colourful procession*

Kollam

Kollam (formerly known as Quilon) is situated 72 km north of Trivandrum. It is a typical Kerala market town nestled among the coconut palms and cashew plantations on the edge of the Ashtamudi Lake. It is often referred to as the gateway to the backwaters. Kollam has a long coastline, a major seaport, lakes, rivers and hills–bringing together all Kerala's natural attributes in one district. This ancient port town was known to Marco Polo and had trade relations with the Phoenicians, Persians, Greeks, Romans, Arabs and the Chinese.

The Malayalam era is calculated from the founding of Kollam in the 9th century. The town is also associated with the early history of Christianity. Its traditional industries have been cashew nut processing and fisheries but modern industries including coir, ceramics and aluminium are booming.

Alappuzha

Situated 87 km north of Kollam on the National Highway to Ernakulam is the town of Alappuzha (or Alleppey). Alappuzha is often referred to as the 'Venice of the East' because of the canals that criss-cross this quaint city.

Think Alleppey and fish, copra, houseboats, boat races and serene backwaters come to mind. Several boat races are held here during the harvest season (between July and September). The Nehru Trophy Boat Race started in 1952. This prestigious event is conducted at Punnamada Lake on the second Saturday of every August. Scores of decorated low-slung snake boats known as 'Chundan Vallams' compete for the cup. This event celebrates the seafaring and the martial traditions of ancient Kerala and is watched by thousands of spectators who gather along the banks to cheer their favourite team.

1. Quaint canals that criss-cross Alappuzha

2. A benign smile lights up her wizened face

3. Serene and beautiful, an old church on the backwaters

Each boat has a crew of 100 rowers. Alleppey boasts of long, sandy and clean beaches.

Alleppey is also home to Kuttanad, one of the few places in the world, where farming is done below sea level. Kuttanad is under seawater for a major part of the year. Most of the farmland is submerged as water rises during the rainy season. But during other times the farmland is deliberately flooded in a controlled manner to facilitate rice farming.

Between Kollam to the south and Kottayam to the east lie some of the most enticing scenery of palm-lined banks, quaint water-bound villages and little canoes ferrying people–everything framed in mesmerising greenery.

4. *Kuttanad has the distinction of being one of the few places in the world, where farming is done below sea level*
5. *A houseboat glides across the serene backwaters of Alappuzha*
6. *Low-slung snake boats taking part in a boat race*

Kottayam

Kottayam is an important commercial centre and the heart of the Malayalam newspaper and periodicals publishing industry. It is sandwiched between the serene backwaters of the Vembanad Lake on the west and the mighty Western Ghats on the east. Most of India's natural rubber (latex) is grown in and around Kottayam. Kottayam was the first town in India to achieve 100% literacy and is the hometown of India's first Booker prizewinner Arundhati Roy, the celebrated author of 'God of Small Things'. No wonder Kottayam has earned itself the title the land of lakes, letters and latex.

There are several churches and temples in and around Kottayam representing the various religious communities, which live in perfect harmony here. This peaceful town on the banks of the Meenachil River has a sizeable Syrian Christian population. The St Mary's Orthodox Church of

Cheriapally (which means small church) has an impressive façade and 400-year-old vegetable dye paintings on the walls and ceiling. The Valiapally (big church) and St Mary's Church about 100 m away was built in 1550. One of the stone crosses on the altar has a Pahlvi Persian inscription. Hail Selassie of Ethiopia signed the guest book here in 1956.

Thirunakkara Shiva Temple is located in the heart of the town. This important temple of Hindu pilgrimage is built in typical Keralan architecture. It is well known for its traditional Sanskrit drama, Kutiyattam.

The Shiva Temple at Ettumanur, 12 km north of Kottayam, is famous for its superb woodcarvings and murals, which are almost identical to those found at the Mattancherry Palace in Kochi.

Kumarakom

Kumarakom is a sleepy little village tucked away from the din and bustle of Kottayam, yet only 10 km by road on the banks of the Vembanad Lake, which is a part of Kuttanad, better known as the `granary of Kerala. Kumarakom today is a very famous tourist destination.

A 14 acre bird sanctuary adds to the natural beauty of Kumarakom. Birds such as Water ducks, Cuckoos, Siberian Storkes etc. make Kumarakom their peaceful home.

The waterways of Kerala have played a main role in the economy of the state. Riceboats and small ships used to ply in these waters, carrying coconut, rubber, rice and spices to various trading centres of Kerala. Even today, these waterways link remote villages and islands with the main land. It is an incredibly different experience to cruise in the backwaters in country boats, absorbing the beauty of the villages.

Previous page

1. *The Shiva Temple is one of the oldest Hindu temples in Kerala. People flock here to pray to the Lord. The exquisite murals on the walls of Ettumanur Temple depicting Hindu epics*
2. *Elephants play an important role in temple ceremonies in Kerala*

3. The grand interior of a church in Thiruvalla. Thiruvalla's Christian roots go back nearly 2000 years

4. The terrifying face of Roudra Bhiman

5. Collecting latex from a rubber tree

This page

1. A houseboat cruises along as the passengers relax and enjoy the enchanting beauty of the backwaters

2. Cheriyapally (small church) has an impressive façade. The walls and ceiling of this 400-year-old church are adorned with vegetable dye paintings

3. The waterways of Kerala continue to play a significant role in the state's economy

4. Chendemelam (a drum ensemble) is performed at all temple festivals in Kerala

5. Lush green paddy fields enhance Kerala's natural beauty

Periyar

The Periyar wildlife sanctuary is situated in the Cardamom Hills region of the Western Ghats. It is an idyllic retreat for both nature lovers and wildlife enthusiasts. The Periyar Wildlife sanctuary is spread across 777 sq. km, of which 360 sq. km is thick evergreen forest. This is the only sanctuary in Kerala that offers the unique opportunity of viewing wildlife in their natural habitat at close quarters from the safety of a boat on the lake. A 26 sq. km artificial lake spreads into Tamil Nadu (the British created it in 1895 to provide water for Madurai and Ramanathapuram districts). The sanctuary was created in 1934 and it receives over 300,000 visitors annually. The sanctuary was designated a part of Project Tiger in 1973 but if you are going to see tigers.

The greatest attraction is the herds of elephants that often come down to frolic in the waters. The mesmerising

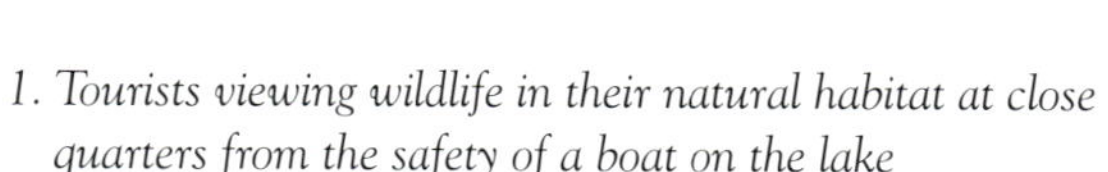

1. Tourists viewing wildlife in their natural habitat at close quarters from the safety of a boat on the lake

2. Great Cormorant (Phalacrocorax carbo)

3. The king of the jungle prowls through the lush green grasslands

sounds of the wild, constant yet soothing chirping of the birds and stimulating aroma of spices is just a hint of the sights and sounds that await the traveller at Periyar.

Bound by evergreen flora and dotted with tall shady trees entwined with pepper vines, this exotic sanctuary is a birdwatcher's delight (over 60 different feathered birds frequent the locale). Situated 2800 feet above sea level, the climate is pleasantly cool through out the year and the unpolluted mountain air truly invigorating. And the experience sublime!

4. Tribals perform a dance in ornamental costume

5. Consider your visit to Kerala incomplete without an elephant ride!

6. Raman, a retired forest watcher, belongs to the local tribal community

7. Pepper 'the king of spices' grows abundantly on the Malabar Coast

8. The Periyar National Park is a safe haven for the Great Indian Elephant

Munnar

A breathtakingly beautiful and scenic drive meandering through forests and plantations 70 km north of Periyar brings you to the tiny hill town of Munnar (1542 m above sea level). Munnar, which literally means 'three rivers', is situated at the confluence of three mountain streams– Mudrapuzha, Nallathanni and Kundla. The former summer resort of the erstwhile British in South India, Munnar is home to some exotic flora including the renowned 'Neelakurinji' the flower that blooms only once every 12 years bathing the hills in blue. The next bloom is in 2018. Formerly known as the 'High Range of Travancore', this hill station is a wonderful alternative to the more popular resorts of Kodaikanal or Ooty in Tamil Nadu.

Set amid South India's most spectacular mountain region Munnar is one of the highest tea-growing centres in the world and the highest peak in South India;

1. The cascading waters of Valara fall on the way to Munnar

2. The perfectly manicured tea gardens of Munnar

3. Gandhi memorial in Munnar obscured by the hoardings and scaffolding

Anamudi (2700 m) is also located here. There are about 30 tea estates that sprawl across these hills. The winding lanes of this quaint town are filled with the fragrance of fresh tea wafting out of the innumerable tea processing plants. Beyond these estates are rich tropical forests that are home to a variety of wildlife including the Nilgiri Tahr, the rare mountain goat saved from the brink of extinction, Nilgiri Langur, Sambar, Gaur, elephant and lion-tailed Macaques.

4. The world's highest tea plantation is at Kolukkumalai

5. A 100-year-old church in Munnar

6. Happy children on their way to school

7. Tender and delicate tea leaves

8. Hills covered in blue by Neelakurinji flowers that bloom only once every 12 years

9. Nilgiri tahr also known as Nilgiri Ibex

10. From plant to pot

Kochi

Kochi, formerly known as Cochin, is a cluster of islands and narrow peninsulas. It is one of India's largest ports and a major naval base. Kochi is one of India's most intriguing cities. It was first and foremost a trading city and still remains the commercial capital of Kerala. Arabs and Jews settled here in the 1st century AD and these communities prospered here under the patronage of the local rulers. In the 14th century when the nearby port of Kodungallor (Cranganore) silted up, Kochi became the most important port on the Malabar Coast. The Portuguese who arrived in the early 1500s dominated the spice trade here till the Dutch gained supremacy in 1663. The British took control just over a century later. Here you can see the oldest church and the oldest surviving Jewish settlement and neighbourhood in India. The ancient temples, churches and synagogues in this district are of special interest to archaeologists and historians.

1. The ingenious cantilevered Chinese fishing nets are be lieved to be the legacy of traders from Kublai Khan's court.

2. Exotic Ernakulam market

3. Jew Town in Kochi is full of history and antique shops; an antique collector's delight

4. The Jewish Synagogue in Kochi built in 1568 bears testimony to the religious harmony that existed in Kerala

5. *St Francis Church, Vasco da Gama was buried here in 1524. The remains were later moved to Lisbon though the tombstone still remains*

6. *The Dutch cemetery where the martyrs of the Dutch invasions lay buried. The Dutch left their indelible imprint on Kochi*

7. *Yet another splendid view of the backwaters*

From time immemorial, Arabs, Chinese, Dutch, British and Portuguese seafarers followed the sea route to Kochi and left their impressions on her shores. It is here that you will find a Jewish community with roots going back to 1000 AD, a 16th Century synagogue, Chinese fishing nets, St. Francis Xavier's Church, where Vasco da Gama was originally buried and Mattancherry Palace. The Portuguese built the Mattancherry Palace and presented it to the then Maharaja of Cochin Veera Kerala Verma. The Dutch extended and renovated the palace. The murals on the wall depict scenes from the Hindu epics.

With a history so rich and a setting so perfect Kochi could be a vacation destination in itself. Famed for its natural harbour, one of the finest in the world, Kochi has earned the sobriquet 'Queen of the Arabian Sea.' Kochi and adjacent Ernakulam reflect the essence of Kerala.

Thrissur

Thrissur, formerly known as Trichur is situated 78 km north of Kochi The word Thrissur is derived from the Malayalam word Thiru-Shiva-Perur which means the town of the Sacred Siva. Thrissur has been an important religious and cultural centre for centuries. The central and most important feature of Thrissur, one of the major towns of North Kerala, is the Vadakkumnatha Kshetram dedicated to Lord Shiva. Thrissur town literally radiates out from the Vadakkumnatha Temple situated on a hillock right in the centre of the town.

The temple is renowned for the Pooram festival celebrated here annually between the months of April and May. The Pooram is one of the biggest and most colourful festivals in South India. Caparisoned elephants and a midnight fireworks display are its highlights.

Located 30 km north of Thrissur in Cheruthuruthy is Kalamandalam, a training school for Kathakali and other Keralan art forms, such as Mohiniattam and Kutiyattam. Like Kathakali, both Mohiniattam and Kutiyattam are classical dance forms with a rich and ancient heritage.

1. Caparisoned elephants are the highlight of Pooram, the most important and colourful temple festival in Thrissur

2. Panchali, this female character is trying to explain her viewpoint in typical Kathakali style. Men in elaborate costume and make up portray female characters

3 & 4. The Kalpathi Temple near Palakkad is dedicated to Lord Shiva and dates back to 1425 AD. The Temple is famous for the chariot festival that is held every November

Palakkad

Palakkad is the land of palm trees and paddy fields. The popular belief is that Palakkad is the fusion of the two Malayalam words, Pala a tree (Alstonia scholaris) which is found abundantly in Palakkad and Kadu which means forest. It is the chief granary of Kerala and is often called the Gateway of Kerala. Palghat lies at the foot of the gigantic Western Ghats, on the border of Kerala and Tamil Nadu. This district with mountains, forests and fertile valleys, rivers and mountain streams is rich in flora and fauna. The Sahya ranges bordering the region and the 20-mile gap in the mountains exert a dominant influence on the climate of the region. Many rivers that flow into the Bharathappuzha arise from these mountains.

Kozhikode

Kozhikode, formerly known as Calicut, is situated 143 km north of Thrissur along the Arabian coastline. Kozhikode was the former capital of the powerful Zamorins. This ancient commercial town has attracted foreign travellers from time immemorial. There are documented visits in as early as the 14th century, by Chinese travellers like Zheng He. Vasco da Gama first landed in India at Kappad near Calicut in 1498 AD and it is believed that the Zamorin himself received him. He was the first European to reach India via the sea route around the Cape of Good Hope in southern Africa. His arrival heralded Portuguese supremacy in India and a turning point in the tumultuous history of Kozhikode. Later the Dutch, the French and the British came to its shores. Thus began a period of continuous conflict of foreign powers for domination of trade in Malabar.

1. Kappad Beach, Vasco da Gama landed here in 1498

2. Bright and happy Muslim children on their way to school

3. The serene face of rural Kerala

Kannur

One of the most important coastal towns of Kerala, Kannur formerly known as Cannanore is situated 317 km north of Kochi and 93 km from Kozhikode.

Kannur has always been a favourite destination of the intrepid foreign traveller. Europeans, Chinese and Arabs have visited its coasts. Marco Polo recounts his visit to the area in 1250 AD. Other visitors include Fahian, the Buddhist pilgrim and Ibn Batuta, writer and historian of Tangiers. The capital of the north Kolathiri Rajas for many centuries Kannur is steeped in history and there are numerous monuments and places of historical interest here.

St Angelo's Fort built by the Portuguese in 1505 is currently occupied by the Indian Army. Moppila Bay is a natural fishing harbour near St Angelo's Fort. A sea wall projecting from the fort separates the rough sea and inland water. During the Kolathiris' regime it was a commercial harbour that linked Kolathunadu with the outside world. Today, Mopilla Bay has turned into a modernised fishing harbour, developed under the Indo-Norwegian Pact. Ezhimala is an isolated cluster of hills north of Kannur noted for their rare medicinal herbs.

The Kadamba kings built Bekal Fort between 1645 and 1660. It is one of the largest and best-preserved forts in Kerala. In the 18th century, Tipu Sultan captured it and occupied it briefly till the British East India Company wrested it.

4. *Theyyam, the ancient ritualistic dance form of Northern Kerala*

5. *Kuttichirapally (Calicut) mosque in the old quarter of Thekkepuram*

1

Karnataka

Karnataka is the eighth largest state in India both in area and population. Formerly known as Mysore state, the name was changed to Karnataka in 1973 to revive the great image of the region, which under the name Karnataka had attained glorious heights in history. The name Karnataka is derived from the Kannada word Karunadu, 'lofty land' and is aptly justified as most of the state is situated on high plateau land. The earliest references to this land are found in the Hindu epics Ramayana and Mahabharata and ancient Jain legends. A brief overview into Karnataka's early history offers valuable insights into its rich culture and colourful heritage.

In the 4th century BC, Karnataka was part of the Mauryan Empire. Around 30 BC, a local dynasty, Satavahanas came to power and ruled the area for about 300 years. Subsequently, the powerful Pallavas of Kanchi (modern-day Kanchipuram) took over and ruled for about a century till the Kadambas took over in the north and the Gangas in the south. By the beginning of the 6th century AD the Chalukyas established a new empire till the Yadavas of Devagiri and the Hoysalas

3

4

of Dwarasamudra came to power and divided Karnataka between them. Around the 14th century, the mighty Vijayanagar Empire was established. The glorious era of the Vijayanagar Empire came to an end when a confederation of Muslim sultans of the Deccan overthrew them at the Battle of Talikota in 1565. In 1399 AD Yaduraya, the ruler of a small principality, Mysore, founded the Wodeyar dynasty. Raja Wodeyar (1578—1612 AD) enlarged the principality into a mighty kingdom, with Srirangapatnam as his capital. Hyder Ali, the intrepid Muslim general of Mysore, overthrew the Wodeyars in 1761 AD. Hyder and his son Tipu Sultan took an anti-British stance, which subsequently led to their downfall and the death of Tipu in 1799 when the British stormed the fort at Srirangapatnam and restored power to the Wodeyars as their feudatory. The British split the state and ruled it under different administrations. Following India's independence, the constant demand of the Kannadigas for a unified state led to its formation in 1956.

Karnataka has witnessed the rise and fall of some of the greatest dynasties India has seen. Invaders from the north largely influenced cultural affiliations and the state's development. Its northern districts saw the rise of architectural styles that shaped the distinctive traditions of North and South Indian Hindu temples. Islam however, spread its powerful influence to the southern most towns and cities. Karnataka has innumerable architectural masterpieces that include well-preserved religious monuments and monolithic sculptures that fascinate every visitor. The Kannadigas are warm, friendly and cultured.

General Information

Area: 191,791 sq. km; Capital: Bangalore; Population: 52 million; Language: Kannada; Literacy: 39%; Best time to visit: October to February; Airports: Bangalore, Mangalore & Belgaum.

1. Commercial sunflower cultivation is a highly profitable business in Northern Karnataka
2. Young Hindu boys are sent to study in a Mutt. The word Mutt stands for a seminary, cloister or religious college
3. An idyllic view of rural Karnataka
4. In rural Karnataka it is not the car but the bullock cart that is the 'king of the road'
5. Portrait of a hardworking farmer

The Geography

Situated on the western edge of the Deccan plateau Karnataka is bordered by Maharashtra and Goa on the north, Andhra Pradesh on the east, Tamil Nadu and Kerala on the south and the Arabian Sea on the west. As it is on the dividing line between the north and the south of the continent, Karnataka is the state where the north and south truly meet. The two most important river systems of Karnataka are the Krishna and its tributaries in the north and the Cauvery (Kaveri) and its tributaries in the south. Both these rivers flow eastward into the Bay of Bengal, the Krishna passing through Andhra Pradesh and the Cauvery through Tamil Nadu.

Malnad or hill country, in the Western Ghats has beautiful dense forests, waterfalls and wildlife parks. The forests of the Malnad region produce teak, sandalwood and bamboo. The coffee estates here grow some of the world's best coffee. Although parts of northern Karnataka are barren, rocky and covered with shrub, the state has a lush coastline with exquisite beaches similar to those up north in Goa, but quieter and more relaxed. The local sport of buffalo racing is conducted with great enthusiasm in the waterlogged paddy fields along the coast.

Highlights of Popular Places

Temples: Aihole, Belur, Halebid, Pattadakal & Sravanabelagola; Beaches: Kundapura, Kudle, & Malpe; Hill Stations: Kodagu (Coorg); Wild Life Sanctuaries: Bandipur & Mudumalai; Historical Site: Hampi ruins.

Festivals

There are several festivals that are common to all the four Southern states. However, there are some festivals, which are exclusive to Karnataka that honour local deities. A few of them are listed below.

January: Krishna, Udupi*; Banashankari Fair,

Banashankari; Ranganatha Swamy, Srirangapatnam.
January/February: Siddheshwara, Bijapur.
February: Virupaksha Swamy, Hampi.
March: Sharana Basaveshvara, Gulbarga; Melkote, Mahabaleshwara (Sivaratri), Gokarna; Vairamudi.
April: Thondada Siddhalingeswara, Gadag; Dharmaya, Bangalore.
October: Dussehra, Mysore.
November: Basavanna, Bangalore; Manjunatheshwara, Dharmastala; Mookambika, Kollur; Gomateswara, Sravanabelagola - celebrated once every 12 years. The last held in 2005.
*Festival/s celebrated every second year.

1. Red-hot chillies being harvested

2. Tender coconuts, nothing quenches your thirst better

3. The ubiquitous banana on sale in a market in Bangalore

4. Followers of the Jain faith offering prayer at Sravanabalagola

5. Her dazzling smile outshines her jewellery

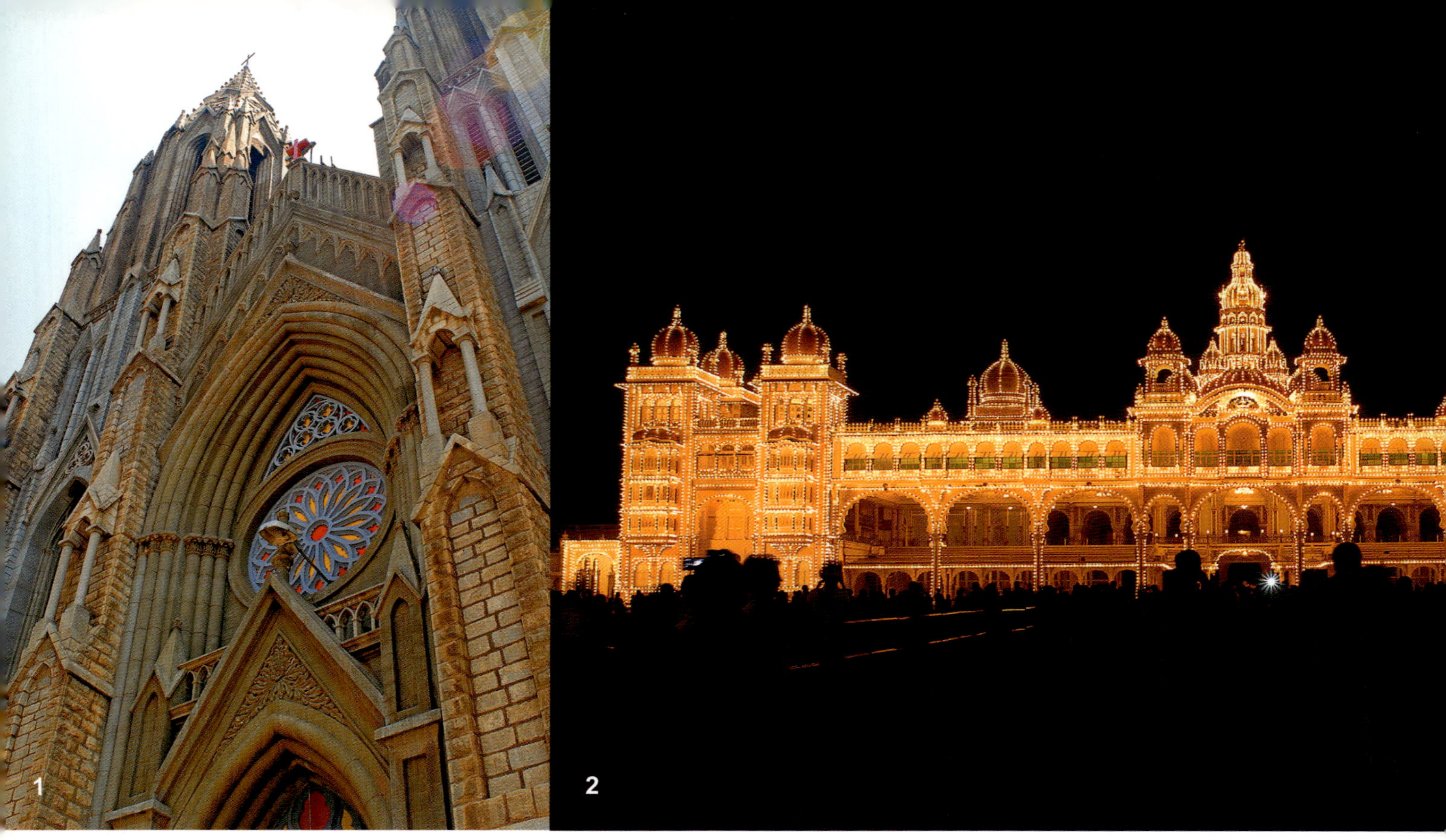

Mysore

The Mysore Palace was the official residence of the Royal family (Wodeyars). The former maharaja is still in residence at the back of the palace.

The palace was commissioned in 1897 after a fire burnt down the old wooden palace. Henry Irwin a renowned architect of British India designed this beautiful Indo-Saracenic palace; the seat of the maharajas of Mysore. It was built at a cost of over rupees 4.2 million and was completed in 1912. One of the largest palaces in the country, inside it is a kaleidoscope of stained glass, mirrors, gilt, wall paintings and ivory inlaid doors. The solid gold throne studded with jewels is put on display only during the Dussehra festival. This superbly maintained palace even has a selection of temples within its grounds including the Shweta Varahaswamy Temple.

The main rooms of the palace are open to the public every day from 10.30 am to 5.30 pm. The residential museum (including some of the palace's living quarters) is also open for an additional charge. On Sunday nights and during the entire Dussehra festival, 97,000 electric bulbs illuminate the building in a spectacular display between 7 and 8 pm.

The Jayachamarajendra Art Gallery in Mysore is considered one of the best art galleries in South India because of its excellent collection of paintings and artefacts that once belonged to the Wodeyars of Mysore. The Art Gallery has been housed in the Jaganmohan Palace (just west of the Mysore Palace) since 1875. It was originally built in 1861 as a royal auditorium. It has a collection of Wodeyar memorabilia, including fascinating musical machines, rare instruments and paintings by Raja Ravi Varma and Nicholas Roerich.

Ten kilometres uphill on the summit of the Chamundi Hill is the Sri Chamundeswari Temple dedicated to the favoured

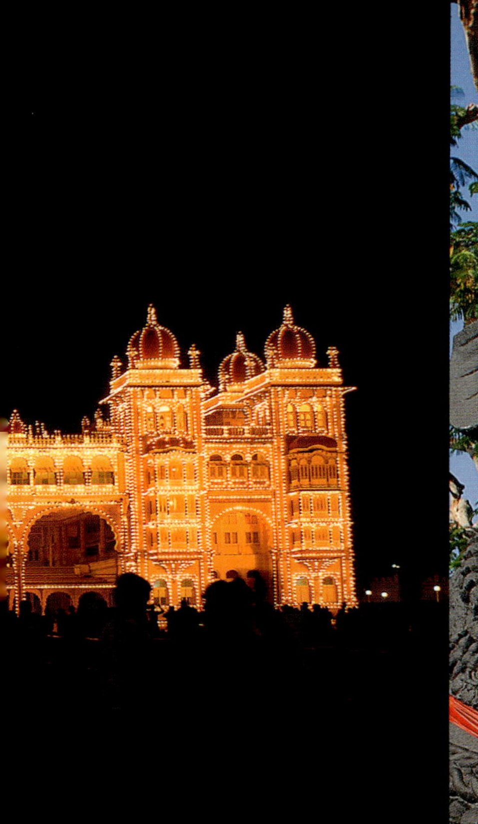

1. St Philomena's Cathedral: an imposing monument with its lofty towers and stained glass windows
2. An extravagant display of lights at the majestic Mysore Palace
3. A Saivite (follower of Lord Siva) priest worshipping Nandi (the bull)

3

1

2

deity of Mysore, goddess Chamundi (believed to be a manifestation of Shakti). Legend has it that Chamundeswari, or Durga (the fierce form of Shakti) vanquished the demon Mahishasura. The temple features a richly engraved seven-storey gopuram. The image of the goddess is made in pure gold and the entrance to the shrine in pure silver. There are around 1000 steps in all, and climbing the first 400 or so steps takes some effort. Enroute to the top, the steps pass the large monolithic statue of Nandi the Bull. Nandi is the vahana (vehicle) of Lord Shiva.

St. Philomena's Cathedral

St. Philomena's Cathedral, only in India can one come across a French statue of a Greek saint in a German cathedral . The Cathedral was built in the neo-gothic style between 1933 and 1941 and is one of the largest churches in India. It is an imposing monument with stained glass windows and lofty towers. The Church has the relic of the 3rd century Greek saint Philomena that is in a beautiful catacomb below the main altar.

Devaraja Fruit & Vegetable Market

Stretching along the Sayaji Road is one of the most colourful bazaars in India. It is indeed well worth a visit and it provides excellent subject material for photographs.

Srirangapatnam

About 16 Km northeast of Mysore, on the Bangalore road, Srirangapatnam is an island town surrounded by the Cauvery. Here stand the ruins of the fort capital from which Hyder Ali and his son Tipu Sultan ruled during the 18th century. The defeat of Tipu referred to as the 'Tiger of Mysore' by the British in 1799 marked the beginning of British territorial expansion in southern India.

The famous Sri Ranganatha Temple originally built in the 9th century is located within the fort.

1. The opulent Lalitha Mahal Palace at Mysore
2. A colourful street market in Mysore
3. Dozens of luscious mangoes waiting to be sold
4. Kili jyothisham is a rather unusual way of finding out what the future has in store. Trained parrots pick up special cards that are interpreted by the jyothish (astrologer)
5. The magnificent Mysore Palace is the city's most popular tourist attraction
6. The monsoon lashes Agumbe, which receives the maximum rainfall in South India

Dedicated to an avatar of Lord Vishnu after whom the town is named, the inner hall of this wonderful temple is the most impressive. Supported by massive pillars, it offers a clear view of the reclining deity in the sanctum.

There are a number of historic sites including the Dungeon where Colonel Baillie was defeated, the Water Gate where Tipu met his end, the Daria Daulat Bagh, the magnificent summer palace of Tipu and the impressive Gumbaz or mausoleum where Tipu was buried.

About 3 km away is the lovely Ranganathittu Bird Sanctuary set around a handful of tiny islands in the Cauvery River. Rowboats are available here for rent.

Somnathpur

Somnathpur is a tiny village 33 km east of Mysore and 32 km southeast of Srirangapatnam. It is famous for its remarkable Keshava Temple and the only compete one of about 80 Hoysala temples in Mysore. The Hoysala King Narasimha III built it in 1286 AD. It has three sanctuaries and stands in the middle of a courtyard with cloisters containing 64 cells around it. The eastern gateway offers a superb view of the temple standing on a raised platform in the form of a 16-pointed star, with an ambulatory.

Beautifully sculpted images of gods, goddesses, and scenes from the epics, as well as the remarkably ornate ceilings in the pillared hall will take your breath away. The temple is open daily between 9 am and 5 pm and is well worth a visit as it is only about an hour by bus from Mysore.

1. A view of the Keshava Temple at Somnathpur, which was built it in 1286 AD by the Hoysala king Narasimha III

2. This fruit vendor even manages a smile for the camera despite the heavy load on her head

3. Intricately sculpted images of gods/goddesses at Keshava Temple

3

Bangalore

Bangalore often referred to as 'The Garden City' for its numerous parks and avenues of jacaranda, gulmohar and cassia is the sixth largest and one of the cleanest cities in India. World-class technological excellence has earned it the sobriquet, India's 'Silicon Valley' and today it rivals Chennai as the most important metropolis in the south thanks to India's booming computer software industry most of which is based in Bangalore.

Founded by Kempa Gowda in 1537 it was also a British garrison town for about 50 years from 1831. Sadly the dramatic growth of the city in the last three decades has almost completely destroyed its architectural heritage. The colonial style bungalows with big gardens in front have almost all given way to high-rise commercial buildings and apartments. Only the High Court and The Bangalore Club have survived till date.

Bangalore is where India's Pub culture began and it still reigns supreme as India's Pub capital. Flashy bars, well-lit discos, pubs serving draught beers and a number of exclusive nightclubs frequented by the city's youth and office goers make Bangalore surprisingly different from the more laid back cities of the south. Excellent shops and cinemas, a variety of places to stay and dine, a convenient transport network, salubrious climate, all contribute to making a couple of days stopover at Bangalore well worth its while.

Whitefield

Whitefield is located to the northeast of Bangalore and is well known for being Sai Baba's summer ashram 'Brindavan'. Sai Baba is the charismatic spiritual guru, religious leader, Godman (to some), social worker and philosopher with millions of devotees spread around the globe.

Nrityagram

Nrityagram is about 30 km northwest of Bangalore. It was set up under the auspices of the late Odissi dancer Protima Gauri to revive and preserve Indian classical dance forms. It is a unique institution, which follows the age-old Gurukul tradition. In the Gurukul system the student imbibes knowledge while residing with the teacher like a family member.

Bannerghatta National Park

Bannerghatta National Park is a national park, which is home to a small population of leopards. A 'safari' is staged here where you can see lions, tigers and elephants in a fenced-in area.

1. Bangalore museum, one of the oldest museums in India, is well worth a visit

2. Brigade Road Bangalore, a wonderful place to hang out

3. Shopping Malls like the Forum provide a unique shopping experience for India's burgeoning middle class

4. Freshly roasted spicy corn for sale. Street food is still very popular in India!

5. Bangalore is a shopper's paradise. Make sure your wallet is well stocked!

Coorg

Madikeri is the capital town of Kodagu district. This elevated charming town formerly known as Mercara is an excellent base to enjoy the Kodagu countryside. Kodagu, which means dense hill country, is the smallest district in Karnataka and is spread over a delightful area in the Western Ghats, with rolling hills, forests, coffee plantations and exhilarating hiking opportunities.

Siddapur is located in the Kodagu heartland and is an excellent place to base your self to explore this charming district.

The Kodagu's or Coorgi's, as they are better known have a unique culture and are fiercely independent. They are best known for their coffee, beautiful women and high-ranking military officers. Believed to be descendants of migrating Persians and Kurds they are proud of their martial traditions and are very hospitable. They also have a distinctive cuisine, in which pork curry (Pandhi Curry) and rice dumplings (Kadumbuttu) are all time favourites.

Tibetan Settlements

Tibetan refugees have settled in India in their thousands since 1959, when the Tibetan spiritual leader, the Dalai Lama, and many of his followers fled to northern India to escape a Chinese crackdown. There are a number of Tibetan refugee settlements in the hills west of Mysore dating back to 1960. Bylakuppe is one of their main settlements with the largest Tibetan population in India, complete with a Tibetan monastery with 7,000 monks, a Tibetan village and a flea market. The expansive halls in the Namdroling Monastery hold 40 ft.-high idols of the Buddha and his disciples. It is a colourful, spiritual, friendly and vibrant place. The Tibetan community has grown and created a niche for themselves here. After the Chinese invasion of Tibet and the destruction of the majority of the monasteries in Tibet, Sera monastery was reformed in Bylakuppe.

Nagarhole

Situated 63 km from Madikeri is Nagarhole, also known as Rajiv Gandhi National Park. Once the favoured hunting grounds of the Maharajas, this pleasantly cool reserve forest on the gentle hills bordering Kerala between Mysore and Madikeri, covers an area of 643 sq. km and was established in 1955. Plantations of teak, rosewood, bamboo, sandal, silver oak trees, eucalyptus and coffee cover most of the area of the park. Home to tribal people such as the Jena Kurumbas, the park is far quieter than others and is a great place to relax for a couple of days. The River Kabini, a tributary of the Cauvery, flows through these forests and the wildlife here includes elephants, wild dogs, tigers, leopards, barking deer, common Langur apart from over 250 species of birds.

Hiking inside the park is strictly forbidden and visitors are permitted to travel around only in the official tour bus. The park is open to visitors from 6 am to 5.30 pm. There are a few resorts and bungalows in and around the park, which offer rustic yet luxurious accommodation. The best time to visit is during late summer between April and May although the most comfortable time is during winter, between November and February.

1. *A Coorgi couple in colourful, elegant, ethnic costume*
2. *The halls in the Namdroling Monastery at Bylakuppe hold 40 ft.-high idols of the Buddha and his disciples*
3. *A Buddhist monk in Bylakuppe*
4. *Red and green clusters of coffee beans*
5. *A herd of elephants grazing at Nagarhole National Park*
6. *The main entrance to Nagarhole National Park*
7. *Chitel, a type of Asian deer with a distinctive white-spotted coat*
8. *The Sambar deer is the most commonly found deer species in India*
9. *The Gaur (Indian Bison) is an endangered species*

Kabini

Nestled in the southern fringes of the Nagarhole National Park, the Kabini River is a perfect getaway for nature lovers. The breathtaking locale with the tranquil backwaters of the River Kabini provides an ideal setting for a long-awaited vacation. Kabini is pure elephant country as one can see numerous herds at a time. However, the blaze of the elusive tiger always haunts you as you roam through the verdant jungle here. Once widely known for the mass elephant-trapping operations called 'Khedda', Kabini stands as the one of the brightest beacons for wildlife preservation in India today.

Perhaps nowhere else in India can one see so much wildlife? Sighting of elephants, sambhar, spotted deer, gaur, wild boar, sloth bear, wild dogs and birds are almost assured. The lucky traveller could even sight a tiger or a panther.

1. *With its dense green forests teaming with wildlife, Kabini is a perfect getaway for nature lovers*
2. *Painted Stork ((Mycteria leucocephala) flourish in Kabini.*
3. *Kabini is pure elephant country and one is bound to see numerous herds at a time*
4. *A Great Cormorant (Phalacrocorax carbo) surveys its habitat*

Bandipur National Park

Established in 1931, the Bandipur National Park forms part of the Nilgiri Biosphere Reserve and is joined to the Mudumalai National Park in Tamil Nadu. It is predominantly a deciduous forest with over 50 species of trees and over 200 varieties of flowers. Tigers, jackals, Sambar, barking deer, mouse deer, wild dogs, flying squirrels, a large number of monkeys, wild elephants and over 200 different species of birds including the great Indian horned owls inhabit this National Park.

The best time to visit is between March and April although the most comfortable time is between November and February. Hiking is not permitted inside the park. Bandipur is easily accessible as it is well connected to Mysore and Ooty by bus. One could comfortably visit the Park for a day from Mysore, which is only 80 km away. There are a couple of luxury resorts around here.

5. *The best way to enjoy the wildlife at Kabini is to take a ride on a boat*
6. *A magical sunset in Kabini*
7. *wild elephants at Bandipur*
8. *The Hanuman or Common Langur (Semnopithecus entellus) gets its name form the Hindu monkey god Hanuman*

1
2

Sravanabelagola

A short 148 km drive from Bangalore takes you to Sravanabelagola, a prominent Jain pilgrim centre in Hassan district. Sravanabelagola is home to Asia's largest monolithic statue–the 58 ft.-high statue of Lord Gomateswara towers here, looming atop the picturesque Vindhyagiri Hill. Every 12 years, Jain pilgrims gather here to participate in the colourful Maha Mastakabhisheka of the Lord, the splendid head-anointing ceremony. Priests pour hundreds of pots of curd, milk, honey, vermilion, coconut water, turmeric paste, and even gold and precious jewels over the statue's head from specially erected scaffolding. Karnataka is endowed with several rich cultural and historical Jain pilgrim centres. The main ones are: Karkala and Venur with huge Gomateswara statues; Mudabidri with the Thousand Pillars Basadi; Humcha with an ancient Jain Mutt; and Narasimharajapura and Belgaum with Jain basadis.

The 12th century Jain basadis (shrines or temples) at Bastihalli (about 1 km south of Halebid) are set in a garden enclosure. These basadis have gleaming black stone pillars and carved ceilings.

Dharmastala

The Manjunatha Temple at Dharmastala is a very important centre of Jain pilgrimage. Situated about 75 km east of Mangalore on the lower slopes of the Western Ghats, Dharmastala is frequented by hundreds of pilgrims every day. Buses ply regularly between Dharmastala and Mangalore.

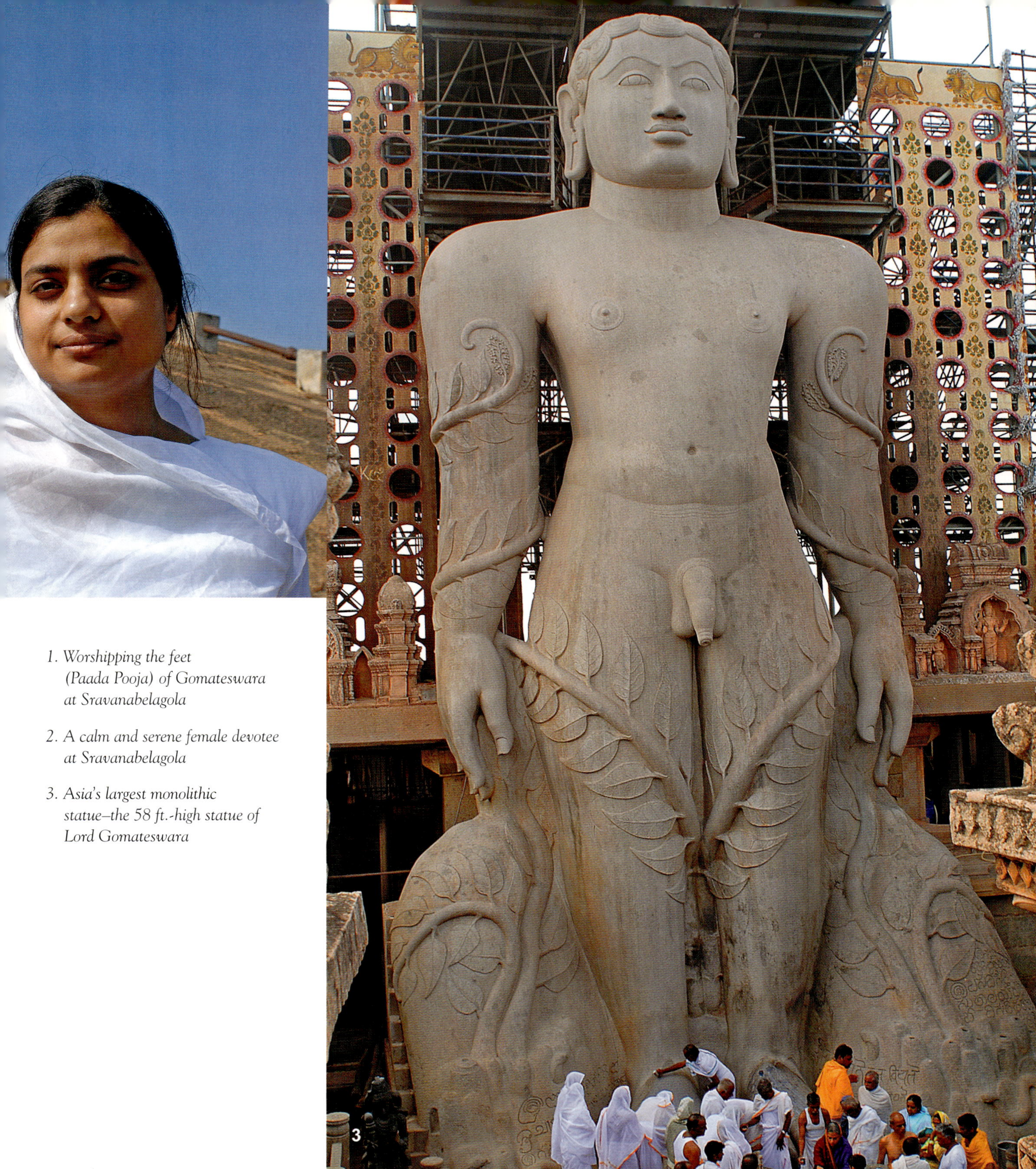

1. *Worshipping the feet (Paada Pooja) of Gomateswara at Sravanabelagola*

2. *A calm and serene female devotee at Sravanabelagola*

3. *Asia's largest monolithic statue–the 58 ft.-high statue of Lord Gomateswara*

1 2

Belur

Chennakeshava Temple, Belur: on the banks of the Yagachi River in Belur, a star-shaped temple with hand lathe-turned filigreed pillars and sculptures will take your breath away. It is the only Hoysala Temple still in active worship. Friezes of charging elephants, each different from the other, mythological figures, military scenes, dancers and musicians, and elaborate decorative motifs charge the imagination. The winged figure of Garuda, Lord Vishnu's carrier, stands at the entrance facing the temple.

The most marvellous specimens of Hoysala architecture, found exclusively at Belur, are the angled bracket figures depicting celestial nymphs. The beautiful and expressive nymphs are depicted singing, dancing or executing daily chores. They are adorned with a wealth of detail in their makeup, jewellery, and coiffures.

The smooth circular platform in front of the shrine displays a sculpture of Shanthala Devi, King Vishnuvardhana's queen. Equally impressive are the temples of Chennigaraya, Viranarayana, Sridevi, and Bhoodevi, all in the same complex.

Belavadi: Belavadi is home to the famous Trikoota Temple, where the idols of Veeranarayana, Venugopala and Yoga Narasimha are located in a single temple complex. It is an excellent example of Hoysala architecture.

1. The front yard of the 12th century Chennakeshava Temple on a bright sunny day

2. A stunning view of the filigreed pillars of the star-shaped Chennakeshava Temple

3. The priest at Chennakeshava Temple takes time out from his busy schedule to pose for the camera

3

Halebid

Hoysaleswara Temple: just 17 km away from Belur is Halebid, the ancient capital of the Hoysalas. The temple, perched on a star-shaped base amidst lawns, is a sculptural extravaganza. Its walls are richly carved with an endless variety of Hindu deities, sages, stylized animals, birds, and friezes depicting the life of the Hoysala kings. The temple complex has a museum which houses the idols, statues, busts, and sculptures excavated by the Archaeological Department from the ruins. It is open daily from 10 am to 5 pm except on Fridays when it is closed.

1. The Hoysaleswara temple at Halebid was built in the 12th century. It is a masterpiece in architecture, design and carving and attracts visitors from around the globe

2. Nandi (Bull) lord Shiva's vehicle is an essential feature of every Shiva temple

3. *A simple village dwelling in Karnataka*

4. *Colourfully adorned cows. Wonder where they are off!*

5. *One among millions of hardworking farmers who are India's backbone*

6. *Sacks of Chillies being transported the traditional way*

7. *A detail of a wall at Hoysaleswara Temple, Halebid*

Chittradurga

This pleasant little town in the middle of Karnataka is situated almost exactly midway between Hospet and Bangalore. With the fall of the Vijayanagar Empire, the local chieftains known as Chittradurga Nayaks took refuge in the fort. Hyder Ali and his son Tipu sultan wrested the fort in 1779 and strengthened and expanded it to its current form. Following Tipu's defeat by the British, the fort lost its usefulness.

The tiny town, which developed within its shadow, slowly grew to include a bus and train station including a few hotels. The fort has plenty of shady rest spots and there is endless exploring to be done. The Banashankari Temple and the Grinding Stones that were once used to manufacture gunpowder are the main sites of interest.

Gadag

On the main highway between Hospet and Hubli is the market town of Gadag. The town is well known for the stunning temple ruins dating back to (c.973–c.1189) at Lakkundi, located 12 km east. There is a fascinating stepped tank here with an arched structure that used to separate the bathing areas for men and women. The two main temple ruins here are those of the Kashi Vishveshwara Temple and the Nanneshwara Temple.

1. Brightly adorned bulls transporting passengers to their destination

2. Young devotees outside Kashi Vishveshwara Temple

3. Framed in a pensive mood

4. Entrance to Chittradurga fort

4

Hampi

Hampi was once the seat of the dynamic Vijayanagar Empire and the centre of Hindu rule for over 200 years since its foundation in 1336 AD. This empire was perhaps the last great Hindu kingdom before the arrival of the British. Set in a strangely beautiful boulder-strewn landscape, the ruins of this ancient city have a magnetism of their own and are awe-inspiring. It is one of the most mesmerising historical sites in South India.

As the capital of the Vijayanagar Empire, one of the largest Hindu empires in Indian history, it was once an enormously wealthy and thriving city having held a monopoly on trade in spices and cotton. The Vijayanagar Empire reached its height during the glorious reign of Krishnadevaraya who ascended the throne in 1509 AD and ruled for 20 years till his untimely death in 1529 AD at the age of 42. At a time when the Mughal armies in the north were conquering and plundering ruthlessly, the new empire in the south, an amalgamation of the small Hindu kingdoms managed to hold invaders at bay with their unity till a Muslim coalition finally managed to rout them at the Battle of Talikota in 1565 AD and destroy the city. Today only the desolate remains of the once magnificent Hindu empire lay strewn on the right bank of the River Tungabhadra. The temples of Hampi are famous for their large dimensions, florid ornamentation, both in painting and carving, majestic pillars, magnificent pavilions and a great wealth of religious and mythological depictions, including subjects from the Ramayana and the Mahabharata.

Hampi is today a thriving travellers' destination, and most people stay at least a couple of days to soak in the atmosphere and explore the area.

Archaeological Museum

The museum at Kamalapuram maintained by the Archaeological survey of India is well worth a visit. There are fine sculptures and various artefacts that have been excavated and displayed here apart from a fascinating floor model of the original layout of Vijayanagar. The model gives an overall view of the magnitude of the site, which would otherwise be difficult to envisage if you are moving around the ruins themselves. The Archaeological Survey booklets are on sale here and the museum is open on all days except Fridays from 10 am to 5 pm.

1. *Hampi–the world's open museum was the capital of the last Hindu empire of Vijayanagar. The medieval ruins cover some 26 sq km*

2. *The Krishna Temple at Hampi is a symbol of the glorious reign of the Vijayanagar Empire*

About a kilometre from the museum at Kamalapuram is one of the largest temples amongst the ruins, the Pattabhirama Temple. The temple facing east has an impressively pillared mandapam. Four kilometres away is the Malyavanta Raghunatha Temple the sanctuary of which is built around a massive rock that protrudes from the ceiling.

Sacred Centre

The Sacred Centre refers to the areas extending from Hampi village to Matanga Hill to its east. As one enters the ruins from Hampi Bazaar in the west over the Hemakuta Hill is the Sacred Centre of Vijayanagar on the northern edge of the city encompassing the Virupaksha Temple and the Tungabhadra River. It was here, according to Hindu legend that the revered sage Madhavacharya lived in a shrine on the slopes of the Hemakuta Hill and played a major role in advising the formation of a new city.

Virupaksha Temple

Legends claim that the first building erected was the temple of Pampapati, which is the modern Virupaksha Temple. However, archaeologists agree that it was probably constructed on the foundation of an earlier temple. It has two courts with gopurams at the entrance. The main entrance with a 50 m gopuram faces east into a ceremonial and colonnaded street, that exends for more than half a mile, to a monolithic statue of Nandi. The main gopuram believed to have been built in 1442 AD with a smaller second one being added in 1510 during the coronation festival of Krishnadevaraya.

The main shrine is dedicated to Virupaksha, an incarnation of Lord Shiva. To the north is a smaller shrine dedicated to Pampadevi, the protector of the city and an incarnation of Goddess Parvati. Entry to the temple is free every day from 6.30 am to 8 am and again from 6.30 pm to 8 pm.

Hemakuta Hill

The slopes of the Hemakuta Hill, overlooking the Virupaksha temple, house some of the earliest structures, some of them built even before the Vijayanagar times. There is a 4.5 m high statue of Lord Ganesh carved from a single block of stone. To the south is an immense monolithic sculpture of the man–lion Lord Narasimha built during the reign of Krishnadevaraya. The remains of the Krishna Temple also built during this time and located between these two statues, are unfortunately in a state of decay. The view from the top of the hill is well worth the climb.

1. *A congregation of Muslim women of different ages.*
2. *The monolithic statue of Lakshminarasimha at Hampi.*
3. *Fruit sellers expecting brisk business outside the temple premises.*
4. *The sacred and the mundane sit together irreverently in this sign board.*
5. *The Vithala temple at Hampi. Those wheels could spin till they were cemented down.*
6. *A Sadhu (ascetic) clad in soothing saffron robes.*

Vittala Temple

The highlight of Hampi ruins is this 16th century temple, which is one of India's three World Heritage Monuments. The temple dedicated to Lord Vishnu is in an excellent state of preservation although cement block columns have been erected to keep the main structure from falling down. Believed to have been built during the reign of Krishnadevaraya (1509–1529 AD) the temple was never completed or consecrated. Yet its magnificent sculptural work is the high point of Vijayanagar art. Entry to the temple is free on Fridays.

King's Balance

To the southwest of the temple stands a simple stone archway and lintel where the king's weight in gold and jewel was measured annually and donated to the priests. A short distance away on the riverbank are the remains of massive bridge, which was built on hundreds of pillars of granite.

1. An aerial view of the ruins at Hampi

2. Arched corridors and projecting balconies overlook a grand sunken tub at The Queen's Bath

3. Hot 'n' spicy snacks for sale

4. *Rural folk traveling at a leisurely pace on a bullock cart*

5. *A plantation owner proudly displays his green harvest*

Queen's Bath

The Queen's Bath is a square shaped building that seems to have been designed for royal recreation. Inside, a columned passageway runs around a large central bathing tank. The ceilings of the passageway are divided into domes with delicate plasterwork designs. The channel from the aqua duct by which the bath was filled with scented water and the drainage outlet for changing the water can still be seen.

Hazara Ramchandra Temple

This temple sits within its own courtyard and was apparently built exclusively for the royal household. The walls of the courtyard are made of massive blocks of stone cut and interlocked with incredible accuracy. On the outside these walls are covered with numerous interesting relief carvings of warriors, horsemen and dancers. Scenes from the Ramayana appear on the inner courtyard walls,

1 2

and on the temple itself. There are four mammoth black stone pillars supporting the ceiling of the second hall within the temple.

Underground Virupaksha Temple

Located about half a kilometre away from the Ramachandra Temple are the remains of the underground Virupaksha Temple. Although much of the area is flooded, it is still possible to explore a certain portion of the structure.

Zenana Enclosure

The two-storeyed Lotus Mahal is within the Zenana or ladies' quarters, which are screened off by high walls. This open sided pavilion seems to have been the reception area. There is an impressive domed Elephant Stable but the watchtower is in ruins. The enclosure is thought to have contained a number of buildings used exclusively by the royal women.

Pattadakal

The second capital of the Badami Chalukyas, the village of Pattadakal situated 20 km from Badami was used in particular for the royal coronation ceremonies. There are numerous temples here with the remains of the earliest ones dating back to the 3rd and 4th century. The most important monuments here are the Mallikarjuna Temple and the Virupaksha Temple.

Aihole situated about 43 km from Badami was the regional capital of the Chalukyas between the 4th and the 6th centuries. It is a picturesque village on the banks of the Malaprabha River. There are as many as 10 temples of ancient origin that are excellent examples of Hindu medieval architecture. The Durga Temple in the centre of the village is the most impressive. It is often noted for its semicircular apse, which indicates the influence of Buddhist architecture. There is a Museum behind the temple, which houses numerous Chalukyan sculptures.

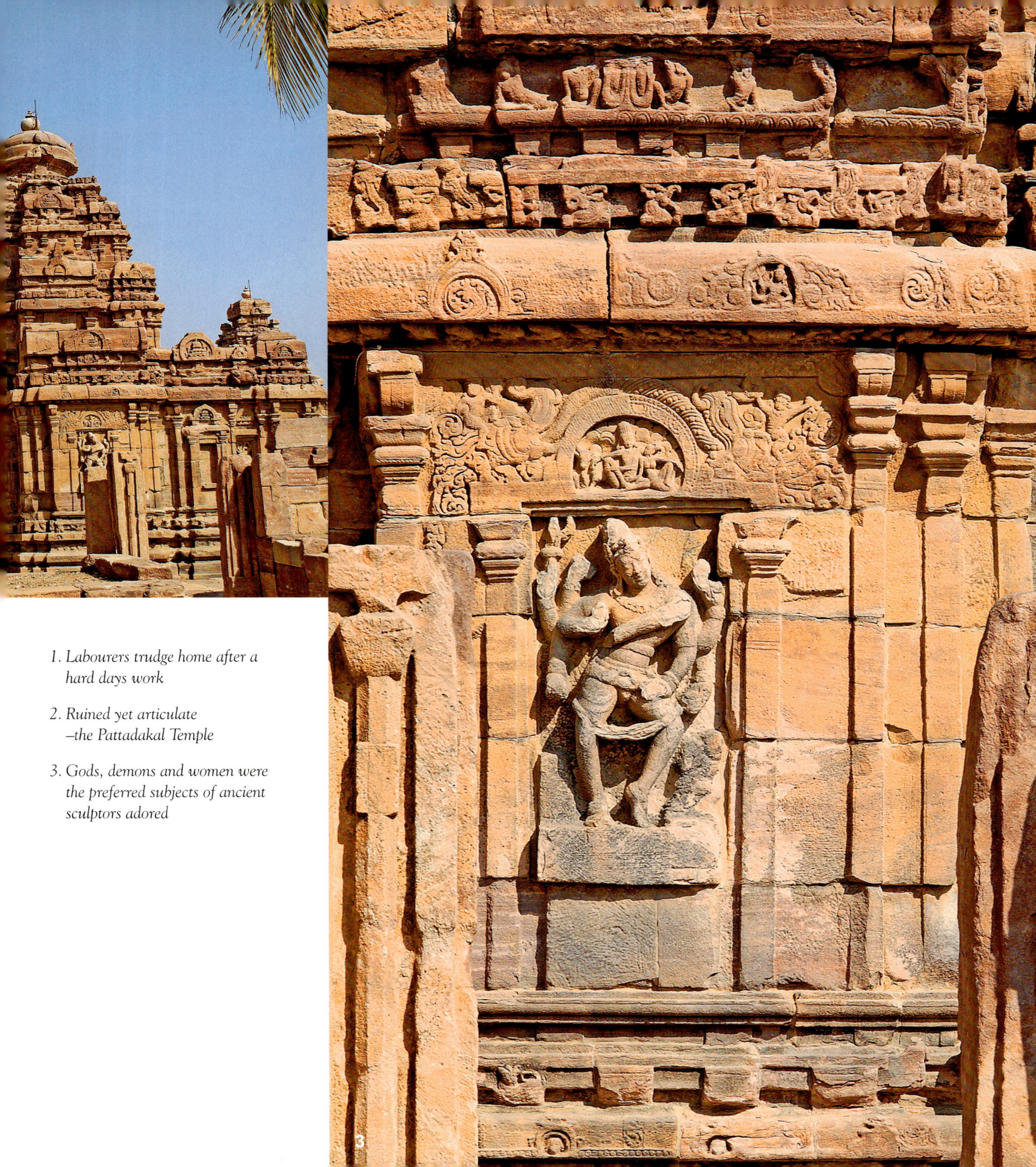

1. *Labourers trudge home after a hard days work*

2. *Ruined yet articulate –the Pattadakal Temple*

3. *Gods, demons and women were the preferred subjects of ancient sculptors adored*

3

1

2

Badami

Squeezed in a gorge between two red sandstone hills, the rural town of Badami is indeed set in beautiful countryside. During the 4th and 8th centuries AD, Badami was the Capital of the Chalukyan Empire. The sculptural legacy left behind by the Chalukyas include some of the finest examples of Dravidian Temples, rock-cut caves as well as the earliest structural temple in the country.

The town is best known for its beautiful caves within the South Fort. Cave one is dedicated to Lord Shiva, Caves Two & Three are dedicated to Lord Vishnu and Cave Four is dedicated to Jainism. Each of these caves is well worth exploring and provide a fascinating insight into the culture of ancient Dravidians. There is the peaceful Budhanatha Temple in a natural cave close to the Agastya Lake, the waters of which are believed to cure illness.

4

1. A red sandstone cliff, riddled with temples carved into rocks, overlooks the Agastya Lake
2. A relief from one of the four caves temples at Badami
3. A view of the exquisite sculptures that adorn the rust red sandstone cliffs
4. Washing can be fun they say
5. A solitary peasant in his colourful headgear.
6. Not a bad way to earn a crust

At the northwestern corner of the lake is the Archaeological Museum where you can find excellent examples of local sculptures and various artefacts. Within the fortified North Fort are the two Shivalaya Temples. The Malgatti Shivalaya Temple stands isolated on a rocky projection above the village.

Most travellers arriving at Badami tend to use it as their base as they explore the neighbouring places of interest as listed below. There is an adequate though limited range of accommodation and the atmosphere is relaxed and laid back. There is a good network of rail and bus services to Bangalore, Bijapur, Hospet and Gadag. The best way to explore the town is by local buses, which operate an efficient service between Badami and its surrounding places of interest.

Banashankari is a small village 5 km away from Badami, and is famous for its annual festival held here usually in January at the local temple. Mahakuta Temple situated 10 km from Badami is another remnant of the Chalukyan rule. This is an important place of pilgrimage as sage Agastya lived here.

1. A fine piece of sculpture inside one of the cave temples at Badami, which are famous for their architecture

2&3. In Badami, the silent stones speak a thousand words

3

Bijapur

Bijapur was a part of the kingdom of the erstwhile Chalukyas of Badami till the end of the 12th century when they were overthrown. Bijapur changed many a hand before falling into the hands of the Bahmani Sultans who ruled northern Deccan from their capital in Gulbarga.

The modern city of Bijapur is a run-of-the-mill unexciting place where the local population move around seemingly oblivious of the multitude of ancient architectural wonders that lay haphazardly scattered around. Bijapur has the feeling of a North Indian Muslim city with its array of mausoleums, mosques and Mughal palaces.

In 1489 the governor of Bijapur, Yusuf Adil Khan who later came to be known as Adil Shah declared independence and founded his own dynasty. Nine Sultans of the Adil Shahi dynasty ruled Bijapur of whom the most notable were Ali I, Ibrahim II and Muhammad.

1. *The Gol Gumbaz at Bijapur is the mausoleum of Mohammad Adil Shah. The dome has an internal diameter of 38 m and is second only to that of St. Peters in the Vatican City*
2. *The scorched earth has little to offer these hungry hordes*
3. *Adil Shah's claim to fame–the Gol Gumbaz*
4. *Golden heads swaying in the wind*
5. *This is how traditional married women dress in rural Karnataka*

3

The reign of the Adil Shahis lasted till 1668 when Emperor Aurangzeb overthrew Sikhandar Adil Shah and put an end to the dynasty. Thereafter the Nizams, Marathas and finally the British ruled Bijapur.

The most notable is the Golgumbaz, the dome of which is the second largest in the world. The famous and most striking monument in Bijapur the Golgumbaz is rather a simple building, which has four walls that enclose a majestic hall 104 sq. m in area supported by octagonal seven-storied towers at each corner. The enormous dome that covers the building has an internal diameter of 38 m, and is said to be the world's second largest after St Peter's in the Vatican.

Om beach, Gokarna (also spelt as Gokarn or Gokaran), Karnataka. The beach gets its name because it is shaped like the auspicious Om symbol; two arcs of sandy beach separated by a rocky outcrop. Om beach is accessible by foot from Gokarna.
A trek across the rocky headland and Cudle Beach will bring one here.
Further south are Half Moon Beach and Paradise Beach, which are popular with western backpackers and budget travellers. The nearby town of Gokarna is one of Hinduism's most sacred sites in South India.

GRT Grand

120, Sir Thyagaraya Road, T. Nagar, Chennai - 600 017, Tamil Nadu.

GRT Grand is the 4-Star Business Hotel in Chennai, with all the facilities and ambience of a 5-Star hotel. Strategically located in the center of Chennai city, GRT Grand combines international standards of efficiency with renowned south Indian hospitality.

GRT Grand is conveniently located in the center of Chennai, near the Teynampet junction just off Anna Salai, 11 km away from the airport and 7 km from the Central railway station.

Phone:+91-4428150500/5500/1617,Extn:1166,Fax:+91-4428150778,
TollFree:1800 4255 500,Email:reservations@grtgrand.com
www.grthotels.com

GRT Temple Bay

A GRT leisure hotel, Mamallapuram 603 104, Tamil Nadu.

GRT Temple Bay is a beach resort intelligently designed to offer the best of comfort and leisure for tourists. The resort also doubles up as ideal location for your business needs, be it conventions, conferences and training & development programs.

Situated at the scenic, historic seaside town of Mamallapuram. Located 65 Km away from the city of Chennai, Tamil Nadu, Temple Bay resort houses elegantly furnished, luxurious rooms and cottages all designed to give you a view of the azure sea, and the legendary Shore Temple.

Phone: +91-4114-243636, Fax:+91-4114-243838, Email:mail@grttemplebay.com
www.grthotels.com

GRT Regency - Kanchipuram

487, Gandhi Road, Kanchipuram, Tamil Nadu.

The franchise of GRT Regency now extends as far as Kanchipuram, providing you with a wealth of hospitality and fine service. GRT Regency caters to the business traveller as well as the regular visitor with a finest restaurant as well as banquet and conference facilities.

GRT Regency, Kanchipuram is located 2 km from the Railway Station and 75 km from the Chennai International Airport. Kanchipuram finds itself in the neighbourhood of the 7th Century Kailasanatha Temple, Ekambareswarar Temple with a 180-foot high gopuram.

Tel: +91- 44 -27225250, Fax: +91- 44- 27224263, Email: adminkanchi@grtregency.com
www.grthotels.com

Chettinadu Mansion

S.A.R.M. House, T.K.R. Street, Kanadukathan, Sivaganga District, Tamil Nadu.

This 100 year old architectural marvel is situated in Chettinadu, one of the Hidden Treasures of TamilNadu. It's 126 rooms and sheer size of the marriage hall, tall pillars, beautiful balconies, and hidden lofts the size of a large room in the false ceilings are features typical of a by gone era of gracious living. Chettinadu Mansion is a Heritage Home bringing to its privileged clients the living style of the Chettiars.

Chettinadu situated 2 hours away from Tiruchy, Tanjore and Madurai.

Phone:+91 4565 273080, +91 94434 95598 Email: info@deshadan.com
www.chettinadumansion.com

Sterling Swamimalai

Thimmakudy Village, Baburajapuram Post, Kumbakonam-612 302, Tamil Nadu.

The 1896 villa radiates harmony and depicts South Indian life style. One gets automatically transported to the period 1896. Sterling Swamimalai is a confluence of Leisure, Heritage, Health, Nature, Aesthetics, Spirituality, Fine arts and Fun, that creates harmony for the body, mind and soul, offering each guest authentic South India experience.

Sterling Swamimalai, the 100 year old Heritage home with period interiors is located in a beautiful coconut grove on the banks of River Cauvery near Tanjore.

Phone: +91-435-2480044 Fax:+91-435-2481705, Email: info@indecohotels.in
www.sterlingswamimalai.net

Hotel Malligi

T6/143, J. N. Road, Hospet - 583 201, Karnataka

Hotel Malligi, is beautifully spread over 5 acres of land in the heart of Hospet. It can be reached within minutes as soon as one steps into the city.With more than 25 years of experience in the trade of hospitality, we at Malligi have attended and served to each and every need of domestic and foreign tourists to make their stay enjoyable and memorable.

Phone : +91- 839 4228101 Fax : +91 839 4227038 E mail: malligihome@hotmail.com
www.malligihotels.com

Ivory Tower

Penthouse Floors, Barton Centre, 84, M.G.Road, Bangalore-560001

Ivory Tower is an all suite hotel located on Bangalore's vital business artery, Mahatma Gandhi Road. Perched on the top two penthouse floors of Barton Center the hotel offers the convenience of location while still promising you a peaceful stay. The hotel has just 18 suites, ensuring that your stay is an intimate experience. The rooms are spacious and sumptuously appointed with a breath taking view of the city sprawled at your feet. Appointed with all the amenities required by modern-day traveller, the lodgings here are designed for the discerning.

Phone: +91-80- 4178 3333 Fax: +91-80-25588697 Email: info@hotelivorytower.com
www.hotelivorytower.com

Orange County Luxury Resorts - Coorg

Second Floor, St. Patrick's Business Complex, 21, Museum Road, Bangalore - 560 025

Nestled in the Western Ghats, perched at 800 meters above sea level and set amidst 300 acres of coffee and spice plantations, is the Orange County Resort - one of India's finest holiday resorts. Come and experience the amazing hospitality of Coorg.

Orange County - Coorg is located 235 km from Bangalore and 4 Km from Sidapur village.

Tel: + 91-80-2532 5302 Fax: +91-80-2558 2425 Email: sales@trailsindia.com
www.orangecounty.in